Also by Richard A.M. Dixon

The Final Warrior
The Crickets of Hiroshima
Inuit
The Tiger of Dien Bien Phu
Dillon's War Trilogy
Angels In My Foxhole

THE
SOUL
OF A
DOG

Richard A.M. Dixon

ISBN 978-1-64300-094-7 (Paperback)
ISBN 978-1-64300-095-4 (Digital)

Covenant Books, Inc.
11661 Hwy 707
Murrells Inlet, SC 29576
www.covenantbooks.com

Foreword

The soul of a human is defined in *Funk and Wagnall's Collegiate Dictionary* as "the rational, emotional, and volitional faculties conceived of as forming an entity distinct from the body." We think of the soul in a religious sense as being confined to the human spirit which lives on after and sometimes before life.

No animals or other creatures need apply.

If that's so, then how does it apply to angels? They surely exist. I know because I have had contact with them. But they are not human. Do they not have souls? Are they not rational, emotional, and volitional creatures of God? I believe that the universe of God's creatures consists of many souls. By observation, both rational and emotional, I believe that dogs fall into the category of creatures with a soul.

This book is about the soul of a dog.
The spirits of my dogs appear nightly as I sleep.
Their warm breaths touch my heart,
and I dream of their presence.
Though their lives have long since ended,
I see their eyes' shining essence.

In the dark, they reach out to me,
lovingly nosing their way into my bed,
licking my face with avid attention
as if they would live with me again,
loving without reserve, their intention.

But though they cannot rejoin me in life,
they accompany me ever
through this life kept warm by their memory
until one day, finished with this body,
my soul joins with those of my canine adulatory.

Introduction

When the Vietnam War came to an end in 1972, there were some two thousand military dogs serving in South Vietnam. Some were trained as guard dogs, protecting American facilities and supply dumps. Others were trained as scouts and worked in the jungles, on point for our soldiers, alerting them to booby traps and ambushes. Many were killed in action. Those dogs surviving when the fighting was finished were turned over to the Army Quartermaster Corps for disposal. They were all euthanized in-country.

Happily, the rules were changed with the advent of the Persian Gulf Wars, and military service dogs who completed their service were awarded full status as retired military veterans. Now they are rehabilitated to civilian life and offered for adoption to live their lives out in peace and loving kindness.

This book contains the stories of two canine war heroes. "Little Joe" was a Japanese Kennel Club, certified German shepherd, born on Okinawa, and killed in action 1966 at the Battle of the Ia Drang Valley, in the central highlands of Vietnam near the Laotian border.

The other dog, "Snake," was an ugly unlovable little Vietnamese cur. He lived and died in the war-torn jungles of the central highlands. He dedicated himself to the service of the Kon Tum District Advisory Team and was killed in action in 1969. He saved my life on more than one occasion.

Neither of these dogs ever set foot on American soil, but they served our country with distinction and deserve to be remembered as fallen heroes.

The other dogs in this story were real, loved our family, and were loved by them all their lives. "Bummer" was eighty-five pounds of half wild malamute and wolf. He helped raise our children.

"Raj" or Tacoma's proud maharaja was a pedigreed German shepherd who grew to 120 pounds. He was the scourge of every vet on Vashon Island, Washington, but he loved us and kept us safe.

"Chloe," a pedigreed golden retriever was the opposite of the other dogs. Where they were aggressive, she was gentle. Where they were independent, she was loving. She saved my wife's life.

And finally, there is "Sandy," a rescue dog from the Tacoma, Washington, center, whom we thought was a golden retriever and turned out to be a Nova Scotia Duck Tolling Retriever. She lives today to serve my wife in her declining years.

I dare you to read their stories without shedding a tear.

Prelude

They say every dog needs a kid. Certainly, every kid needs a dog. My wife Brenda, God love her, speaks fondly of a childhood she shared with a small, white dog she called "Bingo." I had several dogs for short stints when I was a boy. Only one is remarkable, and I had him only for a short while. My father's attitude toward dogs and cats was that they were simply another mouth to feed and he had five mouths to feed during the last years of the depression and during World War II.

"King" was a magnificent English Setter with unbounded energy. He lived most of his early life in a too-small kennel next door to the house where my grandmother lived in Ashland, Massachusetts, during the years just after World War II. We had lived there during the entire war. Both my parents worked in one of the two factories dedicated to defense manufacturing. When the war ended, so did the work, and my family was forced to move into the slums of Boston where my dad worked as a short-order cook. He sought and found a job as caretaker on a twenty-acre estate in Mansfield, to the west of Boston. The caretaker's house was a furnished Cape Cod cottage behind the "big house." Dad had the use of a Ford pickup truck, and on leaving Boston, we went to Ashland to visit my grandmother. Mom and Dad rode up front. My two sisters and I rode in the bed. Leaving Grandma's house after dark, I discovered we had a stow-away—the dog. He cuddled with the three of us in the back of the truck as we sped away to Mansfield, Massachusetts. I believed my dad stole the dog, and I was glad—glad for us and glad for the dog.

I called him "Pal" at first. But when I realized what a fine do' he was, I renamed him "King." Given twenty acres to run free c he ran and ran and ran.

I was in the seventh grade then and took a bus to school each day. Every day, King met me at the bus stop, and we ran together up the driveway to the house. Those are good memories during a time of extreme poverty.

In the summer, the landowners held a party on their front terrace around their fishpond. All was well until King decided to crash the party and jump into the pool. I never knew what prompted him to do that. I only knew the guests got wet and King was in trouble when he jumped into the middle of the party and shook himself off. Dad, however, seemed tickled. We brought King home, and we had our own party.

Dad got fired, and we had to move back into the city. We lived in a basement apartment with no place for King to run. One day, he broke out, and we never saw him again.

I never owned another dog. As a soldier, I learned to think of dogs as individuals deserving of respect. Later, I accepted them as respected members of my family. Never have I thought of them as "pets."

When I was a young lieutenant in the Eighty-Second Airborne Division, my family was as yet very young, consisting of just Brenda, my lovely wife, and my adopted daughter Cindy. On Christmas 1962, I bought her a North Carolina Beagle hound. We called him "Sergeant Major" or "Sarge" for short. This was a sort of parody on our battle group sergeant major who was, true to his breed, the protector of enlisted ranks against the officer corps, owing allegiance only to his commander.

Sarge was a pretty little puppy, with certain fatal shortcomings. We tried to raise him as an inside dog, but he resisted housebreaking to the bitter end. When he was inside, he barked to go out. When he was out, he howled incessantly to come in. Our neighbors, in this physically close-knit neighborhood, were not amused.

It soon became apparent that Sarge had to go. One Saturday, I took him for a ride in the North Carolina farm country and gave him away to the first farmer who would take him.

Brenda cried. Cindy cried. I felt like a heel. I resolved that our family, soon to be four and living in military quarters, could not abide canine attachment. Little did I know what was in store for all of us.

1

I graduated from the University of Washington in Seattle and was commissioned a second lieutenant in the Regular Army in June 1961. I reported for active duty with the Eighty-Second Airborne Division on September 15 of that year. After Jump School, I was sent to Fort Benning for the Basic Infantry Officer Course and Ranger School. While at Benning, I met and married my wife Brenda and took her back to Fort Bragg with me. She had a little girl from a previous marriage. I adopted Cindy a few years later.

Those first years in the Army brought exciting events that separated me from my wife more than I would have wished, were it not for my dedication to the defense of our country. The world presented a series of events, which directly affected the beginning of our growing family.

The Mississippi Race Riots pulled me away for duty on the Old Miss campus. The Cuban Missile Crisis in October 1962 kept me on alert and locked into barracks for some weeks. And then came the beginning of the Vietnam War. My daughter Evelyn was born in 1963. The assassination of President John F. Kennedy in November 1963, while I was out processing for reassignment to the 173rd Airborne Brigade on Okinawa, set the stage for things to come.

An accompanied long tour of three years on Okinawa, then an American protectorate, meant leaving my family stateside until I could procure housing for them on the island. I would search for housing on the local economy until such time as on-post housing became available. It was a painful process. Each step meant waiting out a list while living in bachelor officers' quarters.

We were lucky. We only had to wait three months until a civilian house became available on the Pacific side of the island overlooking the ocean. It was called Awase Meadows and located on a ridgeline between sugarcane fields and cooled by an ocean breeze for most of the day.

I went to see the house. I knocked on the door, and it was answered by a very friendly colonel's wife. She invited me in for iced tea and a look at the house. She showed me about, talking all the while as Army wives are prone to do, seeing so little of their husbands. A big black dog followed us about as we toured the house.

"Don't mind, Jake. He's our guard dog. He's harmless with friends. I recommend you get a dog as soon as you can to protect you from stealie boys."

During my in-briefing by the military police, I had been warned of these gangs of burglars who could break in and steal the rings off their victims' fingers and be gone before they were discovered. They apparently preyed on Americans living off post. On-post housing was too well guarded.

"Please sit down and have some iced tea."

We sat at the kitchen table enjoying the breeze off the Pacific Ocean and drinking cold tea.

"Lieutenant Wargo has a German Shepherd that's just had pups. He may have some left. His wife may be home. Let me give her a call if you wish."

I nodded my head. She dialed the phone.

"Hello, Dianne. This is Jan Carlson. I have a new officer here who's just moving on island. His family will be here soon, and he needs a dog. Have you any of yours left?" She nodded and smiled at me. "Oh, good, I'll send him right over."

She hung up and said, "She's just got one pup left unspoken for. You'll need to go now, that is if you're interested."

"I am and thank you."

Ms. Carlson gave me directions to the Wargo quarters where I met an inquisitive black male puppy who seemed as interested in me as I was in him. I held him in my hands. I wasn't sure he could see. He weighed not much more than a couple of pounds. I looked closely at him. He stared back at me with coal black eyes. I thought about King and Sarge and wondered how a little pup like this was supposed to protect my family from criminals.

"He'll do fine," I said to Dianne Wargo. "But I just signed for a house, and my family isn't due for another several weeks. Can you keep him for a while 'til I'm ready for him?"

"Of course. I understand. We've been through the drill. Besides, this dog needs to be weaned. He won't be ready to go for two or three weeks. If you like him, he's yours."

I picked him up again and held him at eye level. Though I was assured he couldn't see yet, I would have sworn he was telling me, "I think we can make a deal." Then he relieved himself down the front of my fatigue blouse.

"Oh, I'm so sorry," said Dianne.

"That's all right, this blouse has seen worse. I think I'll call him 'Little Joe.'"

"He won't be small for long. His mother and father were big dogs, and though he's the runt of the litter, I think he'll be big as well."

I placed Little Joe on the floor and wrote a check to Diane Wargo while the dog sniffed at my boots.

Brenda arrived at Kadena Air Force Base on a sunny morning during the dry season. I rushed to welcome her and Cindy and little Evelyn, now just beginning to crawl. I was surprised to find Brenda pregnant with our third child. I took them to our new home overlooking the Pacific in the distance and immediately down on a sugarcane field below the ridge on which our house was situated. There were a dozen homes spread along the ridgeline. They were all owned by Okinawans and occupied by American service families. I had spent the last few days hauling furniture from the quartermaster warehouse, trying to make the house look like a home for Brenda's arrival.

She seemed pleased with the house as were Cindy and Evelyn because they each had their own bedroom. Evelyn was crestfallen when she learned she would have to share her bedroom with her new brother or sister.

On the drive to Awase Meadows, I explained the stealie boy situation and that I had bought a guard dog I called Little Joe. Brenda appeared to reserve judgment about that decision.

We settled in for a couple of days before I announced it was time to go get Little Joe. After a call to Diane Wargo, I drove to the Sukiran Housing area to pick up Little Joe. He had grown somewhat and was able to see. He circled me, smelling my legs, and—when I picked him up—smelled my hands and face. Deciding something, he licked my nose. I waited for him to urinate on my blouse, and when he didn't, I thanked Diane and took Joe home.

This was a match made in heaven. The girls loved the dog. He loved them. He ran about the house, smelling out every room. We put down papers for him to do his business on, watched him closely, and moved him onto the papers as necessary. In less than a week, he had the idea and never relieved himself in the house again.

He was a high energy pup. Whenever I came home, duty kept me away, either training in the Okinawan jungles or off island. A lot of the time, Joe would romp and jump into my arms. He began to patrol the house at night, checking on each of the children and sleeping against the wall under the head of the bed that Brenda and I shared. We were introduced to one of the downsides of sharing sleeping space with a German shepherd. Periodically at night, Little Joe would be flatulent. It had us both awake and gasping. We searched for food we could feed Joe that would render him less aromatic.

Joe grew quickly and took on his defensive responsibilities with increasing seriousness. Soon, he began to earn his stripes. One sunny day, most were sunny on Okinawa, I was off training my platoon for jungle fighting. Brenda, in her ninth month, was working in the house. The front door was open to the cool Pacific breezes. Joe alerted her that someone approached the door. It was an Okinawan street vendor.

Brenda faced her through the screen door. Joe, now half grown, posted himself at her side. The vendor waved something at her.

"Oke-san. You buy."

"No, thank you." Brenda backed away.

"Oke-san. You buy," the vendor insisted.

Brenda made to close the front door, and that's when the vendor made a serious mistake. She insisted again that Brenda buy her goods and pulled the screen door open. Little Joe jumped forward and growled, all teeth showing. The vendor beat a hasty retreat down the ridge, never to be seen again.

That evening, as Brenda related the day's happenings to me, we agreed the woman was probably conducting reconnaissance for the stealie boys. We were glad we had Little Joe on our side. My confidence in the dog's ability to keep my family safe was bolstered. I stroked his ears and told him how proud I was of him.

"Joe, you're my best dog." I held his head between my knees and gazed into his dark, intelligent eyes. He looked up at me, tongue lolling, loving me as I loved him. "I love you, Joe."

"Mr-r-r-fff," he said and licked my face, tail wagging.

After that day, I knew I could depend on Little Joe. He showed me in many dog ways that he knew I relied on him and that he'd not let me down. The dog accepted fully fledged membership, not as a pet but as a member of our family.

Our only son Chris was born and took up residence in Evelyn's bedroom. Little Joe started sleeping under his crib instead of under our bed, and we were encouraged by that.

Our family found duty on Okinawa to be pleasant. Cindy started first grade. Brenda was active in the Officers' Wives Club. The children found friends among the neighbors of Awase Meadows. While duty was tough for me, a lot of off-island time, it felt good having my family near.

In the summer of 1964, we faced our first South China Sea typhoon. Married soldiers with families on the island were released from duty to prepare for the storm. We had laid in C-rations to hold us over. Brenda filled the bathtub with drinkable water. I nailed covers over the windows. Joe circled about supervising the preparations. When we were ready, we hunkered down in the living room, listening to the radio. As the storm circled the island for several days, we played games and listened to the rain and the wind buffet our house.

Brenda and I relaxed together for the first time we could remember. We shared our happiest moments locked up in quarters during the storm. Joe gloried in the attention he received. Evelyn, beginning to walk, stuck her finger in his eyes when he licked her face. Chris enjoyed sticking his fist in Joe's mouth and then sucking on it.

After three days, the storm blew itself out, and life got back to normal—as normal as military life got in those times. Vietnam was heating up. The Special Forces Group on Okinawa was rotating its troops back and forth for temporaryin the jungle. Several of our brigade's bachelor officers, anxious to see combat and extra pay, volunteered for duty with the Special Forces.

A Department of Army representative arrived to brief us on our status. The gist of his briefing was that since our brigade was the only U.S. airborne force in the far Pacific, we would be held in theater reserve and could expect to be the last to see action in Vietnam. While I wanted to join the fight, I was content to enjoy my family life on Okinawa. Nevertheless, we junior officers champed at the bit and were anxious to get into the fight against the Communists.

Later that summer, an unfortunate incident occurred. Joe was bulking up, and his body more closely fit the size of his feet. He often ate outside during the day. I had trained him to be cool when a member of my family interfered with his eating in any way. Chris was crawling like a foot soldier under fire. Evelyn was walking and talking like a drill sergeant. I was satisfied Joe was properly conditioned not to be aggressive with any of us.

Cindy was in the yard playing with some of the neighborhood kids. One of them thought to tease Joe by taking his food bowl away. Joe objected by snapping at the offender. The bite, while not serious, broke the skin and caused a major crisis for our family.

Military regulations on Okinawa at the time included a no tolerance policy for dogs. One bite meant ten days in the slammer. A second bite brought death—no exceptions.

I returned home that evening to a fearful family. Brenda told me what had happened.

"Where's the dog?" I looked around but didn't see him.

"He's in the bedroom, hiding under our bed. He understands he's done a bad thing."

I walked up the street to the neighbor's house to apologize for Joe's mistake and make sure the bitten child was all right. Unfortunately for us, they were an Air Force family. It would have been better for us if they were Army and members of our brigade. Their little girl sported a Band-Aid on her forearm where Joe had broken the skin.

"I'm really sorry this happened," I said. "We'll make sure it never happens again."

"I'm sorry it happened too," her father, an Air Force captain, said. "Of course, I've notified the MPs. I'm sure you'll be hearing from them."

"Thanks. Thanks a lot, sir," I said as I walked away.

Returning home, I told Brenda what had transpired and went into the bedroom to console Joe. I coaxed him from under the bed, rubbed him all over, and told him what a good boy he was. At first, he appeared crestfallen, but responding to my affections, he very soon brightened up and walked with me into the living room where the kids gathered around the two of us, wanting to play.

That night, we received a call from animal control to surrender Joe to the post kennels where he'd be quarantined for ten days. I'll never forget the look on Joe's face when I took him to be locked up. The poor dog didn't understand what was happening to him. I knelt and hugged him close, trying to reassure him. He whimpered and licked my face. The veterinary attendant led him into his cell. The dog entered and turned to look up at me. I couldn't stop the tears running down my face. Little Joe barked. I walked away.

The children cried when I returned alone. A member of our family was absent, and we were all missing him a lot.

Two nights later, the stealie boys struck. Unfortunately for them, they tried to enter through the window overlooking the baby's crib. The baby slept well and rarely woke in the night. They woke Chris, and he cried out. Brenda jumped up and rushed to see what the matter was. I lay awake hearing Brenda sooth our young son and, when I heard that all was well, went back to sleep.

The next day, when I returned home from work, Brenda showed me where the screen had been cut. The burglars had failed, but we knew they'd be back. Without Little Joe's protection, we knew we lived on borrowed time.

The day Little Joe was released, we had a party. I stopped at the commissary and bought the biggest steak they had. Joe gobbled it down in seconds. He seemed more excited by the attention we were all giving him. The children were ecstatic. Joe couldn't stop jumping from one to another of us, licking our faces, our hands, and shaking his whole body with joy.

During Joe's first night home, the stealie boys struck again. This time, they cut the screen on our open bedroom window. The first notice I had that something was wrong was when I heard Joe's deep growl followed by a snarl as he charged across our bed and onto the chest of the intruder. Both of them pitched outward into the yard.

I jumped up and ran outside in my underwear, hoping to head them off. I heard screaming from down in the cane field behind our house. I was frantic, knowing the stealie boy was armed at least with a very sharp knife. I called for the dog again and again. All grew silent. It was the darkest part of the night. It would soon be light. I became aware of my near nakedness and returned to the house. Brenda had put on a pot of coffee.

I showered, shaved, and donned starched fatigues and spit-shined boots for the day's duties. Brenda and I sat over coffee as the sky brightened, trying to think of what to do.

"I think Joe caught up with the thief in the cane field just below the house," I said. "I fear that Joe may have killed the thief or the thief killed Joe, or both. As soon as it's light enough, I'll go down there and search the cane."

"Oh, Dick." Brenda was in tears. "What if he's hurt Little Joe?"

"We'll just have to hope it's the other way around."

The sunlight was creeping over the crest of the island as Little Joe ran up to the front door, tongue lolling, and barked. We ran to greet him. I dropped and searched his bloodstained coat for a wound and was cheered to find none.

"If that's not his blood," Brenda said, "then there might be a dead man in the cane."

In the growing light, I descended to the cane field and searched for a body. Though the cane was matted down in several spots and blood was spattered everywhere, there was no sign of a body. Happily, I climbed back up the hill and announced my failure to discover a dead Okinawan to Brenda.

We agreed the whole affair would remain our secret. Little Joe agreed to keep silent. We felt confident we would not be troubled by stealie boys again.

Soon, thereafter, we were assigned on-post housing. We made the move determined to protect Joe from dangerous situations. Henceforth, our family would always include Joe as one of the family.

2

Our lives changed forever in the spring of 1965. Brenda and I had planned a two-week off-island trip to Hong Kong beginning on May the fifth. Instead, I found myself, on my mother's birthday, in charge of a rifle platoon conducting a combat assault landing by C-130 at Bien Hoa Air Base, South Vietnam.

My second rifle platoon—Charlie Company, Second Battalion, 503rd Airborne Infantry Regiment, 173rd Airborne Brigade—was deployed on ninety-day TCS (temporary change of station) ostensibly to relieve Vietnamese combat troops in the defense of Bien Hoa airfield so they could take the offensive against the Viet Cong. We knew it wouldn't be long before we were helping the enemy to die for his cause.

After ninety days, we were supposed to withdraw back to Okinawa. On day ninety, we were notified that we had been assigned PCS (permanent change of station) for the duration of hostilities.

Those of us who had families on Okinawa hoped they would be allowed to remain on the island. We might be able to take leave occasionally at home. I worried that my young family might be faced with having to move stateside without my help. My fears were substantiated several days later when the word came out that our families would have to abandon Okinawa for stateside.

Brigade HQ announced that married soldiers with dependants on Okinawa would be flown home for four days to help their dependants prepare for evacuation stateside. I was worried that my wife would have trouble handling the move with three children, two of them mere babies, and a large dog.

Out of the bush after sixty days of jungle operations and onto a C-130 transport aircraft headed for Okinawa and four days with my family. We landed at Kadena Air Force Base in the early evening. I left the aircraft with several other soldiers on same mission as I. A soft breeze blew in from the South China Sea. I was free of the smell of gunpowder and the sound of rifle fire. It was the closest I had ever come to heaven.

I hailed a skoshi cab at the front gate and headed for the Sukiran housing area. All the cabs on the island were skoshi, which meant small. They were universally prohibited from entering U.S. government property, so I shouldered my duffle bag at the housing area gate and walked up the hill toward home. It was so peaceful and quiet after the chaos of Vietnam after dark. The evening was warm with a cool breeze that blew almost constantly.

I wondered if the little kids would recognize me. I worried that Little Joe might not even let me in the house.

As I rounded the last corner before home, the houses around me emitting cheerful lights through their windows, I could see a light in the near distance I recognized as coming through the front screen door of my house. I heard barking. I saw the screen door pushed open and a dark form moving swiftly in my direction through the gloom. I knew it was Joe, and I knew he knew me. He launched himself at me, nearly knocked me down, and washed my face with kisses. He was grown to full size now, and I was glad he was on my side. As we walked together toward the house, Brenda was suddenly in my arms, and I was home. The kids gathered around us when we entered the front door. Cindy gave me a great hug and kisses. Evelyn gave a shy smile as I picked her up. Chris hung back, his right forefinger and thumb in his mouth. Joe danced around the five of us, tail thumping against furniture.

Later, after a hot shower and a steak dinner, Brenda related how protective Joe had become of her and the kids. He was tolerant of Setsuko, our housekeeper, probably because the children loved her so, but he wouldn't allow anyone else in the house.

We discussed the impending move stateside.

"I don't see how I can manage Little Joe with packers and movers and inspectors and all coming and going," she said.

"I have faith in you, my love. Department of Army tells me my next assignment will probably be to the Advanced Infantry Officer Course at Fort Benning. I want you to go there. I'll make appropriate arrangements for you and the kids to fly to Atlanta. I'll get the paperwork ready to ship the dog and the car. Don't worry about that."

"But I have no family back there now. Where will we live?"

"Here's what you will do. Go to building #1, the headquarters at the fort. Walk up and down the halls until you see stars on a collar. Explain to him that your husband is in the Nam and you need a place to stay for you and your three kids. I guarantee he'll help you get on post."

The four days passed so swiftly, I can't remember what all transpired except we were wonderfully happy and hugged each other a lot. When it was time to go back to Vietnam, we all cried together in the middle of the living room floor. Joe looked so sad.

"Don't worry, boy," I said, as I hugged him close. "I'll be back soon. You'll see."

The next day, I was back in Bien Hoa preparing for search-and-destroy operations in War Zone D. Very soon thereafter, I was promoted to captain and transferred to the First of the Eighth Cavalry in the airborne brigade of the First Cavalry Division located at An Khein, the Central Highlands.

Nine months and fifty or more combat missions later, my name came up for rotation stateside. Brenda had followed my directions faithfully and procured on post housing at Fort Benning, Georgia. She wrote to me faithfully every day, though I only received the letters occasionally and in bunches. She tried her best to keep the letters as lighthearted and cheerful as she could, but one of the letters brought bad news.

She told me that she had been unable to handle all the details of the move plus the children and the dog as well. She was beside herself when she learned that the Army was looking for volunteers for service dogs. She had volunteered Little Joe.

I was saddened but understood her circumstances and wrote to tell her so. I was sure Little Joe would make a great soldier.

One day, just before the end of my tour of duty in the Nam, while participating in the Ia Drang Campaign in the Chu Pong Mountains, I saw a resupply chopper land at our firebase along the Ia Drang River near Laos. I watched a lone soldier dismount. He was led by a dog on a leash. I caught my breath. It was Little Joe. I knew it. I started to call out to him but hesitated. I didn't want to interfere with his training.

He spotted me and recognition flashed in his eyes. Just as quickly, it disappeared as his trainer, sensing his hesitation, chucked his harness and said, "Come on, Blackie, time to go to work."

The dog lifted his head proudly, as I'd seen Little Joe do so often before, and together, he and his handler led a column of soldiers off into the jungle. I watched him go, and just before he disappeared into the brush, he stopped, turned, and looked directly into my eyes as if to say, "I remember you and love you."

My eyes filled with tears. I knew I would never see this beloved member of my family again in this life. My eyes fill with tears again, this time proudly, as I write of this canine hero fifty years later. We, all of us in the family, remember Little Joe with pride. I think of him less like a dog, more like a fellow soldier and combat veteran. His spirit lives on.

I read in First Cavalry casualty reports, after the Ia Drang battle, that among the casualties, a dog called "Blackie" and his handler were killed in action.

3

I returned stateside to a wonderful reunion with my family. The kids were all walking and talking, running and laughing. We talked little of Little Joe. Some of us still felt the pain of separation. I never shared my news of his death until I started writing this story.

As it turned out, my next assignment was to Fort Sill, Oklahoma—not Fort Benning. We packed up and went to Oklahoma and had a wonderful tour together at Fort Sill. After which, we were sent back across country to Fort Benning and the Infantry Officers' Advanced Course. We knew as soon as school was finished, I faced another tour in Vietnam.

I was promoted to major en route to my second tour in Vietnam in 1968. My orders instructed me to report to the Military Advisory Group Kon Tum Region in the Central Highlands of South Vietnam. I was to assume duties as the Senior Military Advisor to Kon Tum District. I was pleased to be returning to this most beautiful area of Vietnam. Its location at the terminus of the Ho Chi Minh Trail, the main communist supply route from North Vietnam into the entire southern region through what was to be my backyard, promised lots of action. It didn't bode well for my longevity.

After several days of cooling my heels in Plei Ku due to continuing attacks on the airfield at Kon Tum, I managed to get through and report to my new commander, Colonel Tom Whalen, a plain spoken Yankee from New England and a man I grew to admire.

He told me my post was located five miles west of the city along Highway 5 toward Cambodia. The highway was little more than a single lane sandy track, but it was a main communist escape route to Cambodia. He also told me my advisory team had been badly beaten up in the last Tet Offensive. My predecessor had been killed in action at that time along with about half his team. Team morale was low. He made it clear I had my work cut out for me.

My assigned area of operations included some 2,500 square miles, the largest district, by land area in Vietnam. The population consisted of some 2,500 Montagnard tribal peoples, about one human per square mile, who spoke various animistic dialects not connected with the Vietnamese language. Most of them understood some dialect of French from the days of French Indo-Chinese influence. They were collected into 110 refugee hamlets grouped in 56 villages under South Vietnamese appointed leadership and all under constant siege from North Vietnamese regular forces, Main Line Viet Cong forces, and local Viet Cong Guerillas. It was altogether a thrilling but dangerous prospect. I had my job cut out for me. I needed to bring my team back up to fighting strength while responding to enemy attempts at infiltrating my district. Colonel Whalen made it clear my first mission was to destroy the enemy.

As the Huey Bravo, equipped with the requisite two-door gunners armed with M-60 machine guns approached for a landing along the one lane road they called Highway 5, I saw that my posting was an old, much-fought-over French outpost. A central building in good repair, the district headquarters, was surrounded by bunkers and barbed wire. The American sector was a compound within the larger compound, defended by a Montagnard rifle company. Neither position appeared particularly defensible.

The Huey circled twice and landed before the front gate of the district headquarters. I jumped out and approached to find the gate open and unguarded. I walked in and looked around. I recognized the entrance to the advisor's compound from pictures Colonel Whalen had shown me. It was the hottest time of the day. No humans were about. In fact, nothing moved. I had been warned to expect siesta at this time. I saw human legs projecting from under the body of a jeep. From the boots and the jungle pant legs, I knew he was an American G.I. Sleeping close by his legs was an ugly black dog that woke and snarled at me as I approached. He was a typical Vietnamese cur about thirty pounds and looked like an undersized pit bull, except as he looked at me, there was something in his eyes that said he would as soon kill me as look at me.

The soldier attached to the boots rolled from beneath the jeep and sprang to his feet. In his hand, he held a sprocket wrench. He was poised for instant combat. He wore a greasy green T-shirt. His hair was dirty blond and disheveled. He sported a broken nose and looked like a boxer who had just lost a ten-round fight to Muhammad Ali.

When he saw my gold oak leaves and recognized I was an officer, he let the wrench slip from his hand and drop to the ground. The dog stood at his side, snarling and showing his teeth. That the soldier did not salute told me he was a combat veteran who would not point me out as a target for anyone watching.

"Burke's the name, sir—Sergeant First Class Burke. I'm the team sergeant here, also chief cook, bottle washer, and head mechanic as needed." He had a gravelly voice and a brogue that could have originated anywhere in the eastern United States. There was something in his eyes that told me here was a man to be trusted, not parade ground material, but to be counted on in a scrap. It turned out I judged him correctly.

I smiled at him and extended my hand. "Dixon's my name. Glad to meet you, Sergeant."

He wiped his hands on a greasy rag and, taking my hand in his, offered a rough, manly response. The dog stood stiff legged beside him, his eyes locked with mine. He growled menacingly.

"He your dog?"

"No-o-o. Can't say he is, Major. Ain't anybody's dog, really. He hangs around me because he thinks I'm the boss. He's kinda the team dog. Anyway, I expect he'll be your dog now."

I gathered this was a longish speech for SFC (Sergeant First Class) Burke. I'd met his like before, veterans of the Korean War on Okinawa and at Fort Bragg, not much for parading but dependable in the field.

"What's his name?"

"We call him 'Snake.' He's good to have around because he smells out VC (Viet Cong). He hates 'em."

"Any enemy of the Viet Cong is my friend. Where is the rest of the team?"

"It's siesta. They're all asleep. The hottest part of the day is the only time Charlie sleeps, so we sleep too."

"How come you're not sleeping?"

SFC Burke shrugged. "I never sleep."

Snake stopped growling and looked up at me with interest. I knelt and offered my open palm for his inspection. He sniffed at it and licked it. I curled my hand around his ugly snout. He jumped back, surprised, and, while holding his ground, looked into my eyes and relaxed. He stretched his jaws in what appeared to be a doggy smile, let his tongue hang out, and wagged his tail.

From that moment on, Snake was my nearly constant companion and tireless bodyguard during a year when I only got a couple of hours sleep each day during the siesta. The remainder of each day was spent mainly with my counterpart visiting various villages and supervising the building of fishponds, schools, and such. The nights were spent waiting and then reacting to VC attacks on our hamlets. As soon as we learned an attack was occurring, I'd call for a Huey to pick me up and take me to the sight of the attack. I'd scope it out and then call in artillery and/or gunships on the enemy.

The first time I called for and climbed aboard a Huey, I was surprised to see The Snake, who had accompanied me to the landing site, jump aboard with me. Jumping onto the canvas jump seat, he settled down and went to sleep. This scenario was repeated nearly every night of my yearlong tour in the Nam.

During the days, he was perpetually by my side and saved my life several times, not by warning me but by striking without warning to counter an attack by an enemy assassin.

Not long after I joined the advisory team, I learned from our medical advisor, Staff Sergeant Grant, that Snake had wandered into our perimeter one night and set off a trip flare, triggering automatic and small arms fire from the local defense forces. The dog was found in the wire the next morning suffering from multiple bullet wounds and near death. The medic had cut him loose from the wire, brought him into the team house, and treated his wounds. Against all odds, the dog had recovered and stayed with the team ever since.

It wasn't long before the dog demonstrated to me why the team called him "Snake."

We were sitting around the team house "smokin' and jokin'" one especially dark night early on in my tour. Light discipline was in effect because we learned of increased sapper activity in our sector. The Viet Cong, VC, Victor Charley, or Mister Charles—as the enemy was variously called—would send sappers to clear lanes through barbed wire and the mined perimeter to gain entrance to our position before attacking. Because we were a likely target at the southern end of the Ho Chi Minh trail, the main avenue of approach from the north, we always were on the alert for trouble.

We passed the time with a game of nickel dime and quarter poker. We played boldly. Our money was "funny money," military issue scrip used in lieu of American dollars.

The dog slept near the door. When he rose and pushed open the screen door, the team alerted. I followed him to the wire where he dropped to his belly and began to crawl forward. I lay just behind him as he faced the wire. I couldn't see anything, but I sensed the quickened beating of his heart. He must have struck because a VC jumped up in front of me, screaming, and jumped away. He took two or three strides and stepped on a mine. A blinding flash of light and a loud explosion deafened me momentarily. I was pinned to the ground. Slowly, I became aware of Snake on my chest, licking my face and mewling like a puppy. I rose and stumbled back to the team house.

"Is there a steak in the house?" I called out to whoever would hear. My brains were still scrambled by the noise and concussion of the blast.

"If there is, serve it up for Snake."

This was only the first of many steaks earned by this canine cobra. Many times, he either saved me or saved our collective butts from destruction.

Needless to say, as each day went by, I counted more and more on Snake's jungle acuity. I couldn't say he was my dog—he was very independent and attuned to the needs of the entire advisory team. We shared a mutual, almost professional respect. Sometimes, I'd catch him sitting close to me, looking up at me, and I'd remember Little Joe.

The most important thing I had to learn in Kon Tum was not to establish a pattern in anything I did. This was a hard lesson to learn because as humans, we are creatures of habit. Doing the same thing at the same time each day meant probable targeting by the VC. Though I worked hard to follow this regimen or lack of the same, I made some important mistakes.

Each evening before dark, I had a habit of working on my HES (hamlet evaluation system) report. It gave my daily assessment and rating of each hamlet's state of pacification, e.g. its state of freedom from communist influence. One evening, as I sat at my desk, working up my report, Snake came whining at my knee. I looked down at him. This was an unusual thing for him to do. I listened. The men were watching a film in the team house. Maybe Snake needed to pee. He knew how to open the doors and could come and go as he pleased. Still he persisted, scratching now at my pant leg.

"All right, boy. Let's go."

We had no sooner left my quarters when a great explosion sounded nearby and knocked me off my feet. The team alerted and hurried to their battle stations at various points throughout the compound. I rose to my feet, ran into our command bunker, and joined SFC Burke there.

"All stations report," I called over the landline.

"Bunker #1 all clear." The four corner bunkers reported in that there was no enemy action. The compound was full of smoke.

"What do you think, Sarge?"

"I dunno."

"I'm going to check it out. Wait here."

The smell of explosives filled the air as I searched the compound. I didn't have far to go when I discovered my quarters blown to smithereens. Someone had planted a Chicom shape charge under my sleeping quarters cum office. They must have timed it to explode during the time they knew I was working on my reports. Force of habit had nearly killed me. Snake had saved me. All my uniforms and other personal effects were destroyed. Thanks to Snake, my bodily parts were all together and functional.

One of the most dangerous habits I formed was to drive into the city each Sunday morning for a weekly regional advisors meeting. The drive, along the sandy track from the district headquarters to Kon Tum City, about five miles, was cleared of mines every morning at sunrise. I made this drive every Sunday alone because I didn't want to expose others to the danger and in time to make the regional meeting. Occasionally, I was ambushed on the road and had to call for help. I could have called for a chopper, but as a matter of pride, I persisted in driving the road each week, though in a randomly selected jeep and purposely without Snake to the meeting.

One Sunday, soon after the attack on my compound, Colonel Whalen, who had become aware of Snake's importance to the team, called me and told me to be sure to bring the dog to the meeting. That morning, Snake stood watching me fire up a jeep to go the Kon Tum. When I called to him to mount up, he leapt to the front seat and sat beside me like a prince as we bumped along the sandy track.

Together, we entered the common room at Kon Tum Regional Advisory Team Headquarters. These meetings were for Americans only. No Vietnamese invited. There were no women. The only American woman present in Kon Tum was Doctor Pat Smith, a Catholic nun from Seattle who ran a Montagnard hospital in the city. She denied any connection with the military affairs of the region.

Snake stayed at my side as I walked about shaking hands with the forty or so advisors and staff members of Kon Tum region.

Major White, the senior district advisor from Dakto, and I, representing Kon Tum District, were the stars of the show since we saw action on a daily basis in the province. We stood together discussing various issues before the meeting was called to order.

"So this is the famous Snake we've all been hearing about," Major White said. "May I pet him?" The dog, usually nervous in a crowd, stood surveying Major White with his cold black eyes.

"I wouldn't recommend it. He's not generally friendly with strangers."

Colonel Whalen called the meeting to order. Snake and I sat together in two chairs near the front. The meeting began with an enemy situation briefing by the region intelligence advisor. He was followed by various other officers who had business to report.

Then it was our turn. Major White gave a thirty-minute briefing on conditions in Dak To. He'd had a bad week having lost two advisors in enemy attacks on outlying villages. When he finished, Colonel Whalen stood and walked to the front of the stage. "Major Dixon will now make his report. He has brought with him the only Vietnamese we've ever invited to these meetings. I asked him to bring Snake because the dog is totally loyal to us and has saved several American lives and is credited with several VC kills. Major Dixon, give your report."

I stood and marched up to the podium. Snake hopped down from his chair and strutted up on the stage with me. He sat at my left, unmoving. He studied the audience as I reported on conditions in Kon Tum District. When I finished and returned to my seat, I found Snake's chair occupied by another officer. I sat down, curious to see what Snake's reaction would be. He had his own chair in the team house—none of the advisors dared sit in it.

The dog pulled up in front of the officer and growled at him.

"What is this?" the officer said.

"You're in his seat. If I were you, I'd vacate."

The officer stood. Snake hopped up into the chair, looked at me with that seeming smile he sometimes offered, chuffed, and sat watching the stage.

One day, early in our association, The Snake—SFC Burke always referred to him as "The" Snake—and I were required to fly out to a remote hamlet and dedicate a new school. We were accompanied by Major Tan, the district chief whose show it was. There were speeches and such, lots of Montagnard people about. It was a perfect place to ambush an American.

As the day wore down to an ending, I sat down the front porch of the new school for a brief rest. I hadn't had my siesta that day.

The Snake sat at my hip, keeping very quiet, watching the crowd. His deep-throated growl caught my attention. I spun, drawing my pistol. I faced a very surprised Montagnard warrior. The Snake had struck the man's forearm baring bone from elbow to wrist. He dropped a machete from his now useless hand and dropped to his knees. I called for my medic who wrapped his arm. "Holy mackerel, Snake sure did a job on this guy," he said.

"Yeah, he saved my bacon again."

I turned him over to Major Tan for processing as a POW. I was never sure the Yard made it to prisoner status.

Snake sat calmly by, tongue lolling, looking very pleased with himself. I was shook up, thinking how close I had come to death.

Major Tan walked up to me. "Tui-Ta" (Major), he said. "I think maybe you betta give dog big steak tonight. He catch big time VC."

"You better believe it, Tui-Ta. He can have my steak as well."

The Snake shook his head and made for the helicopter to settle down to sleep on the canvas bench between the district chief and me for the flight back to district HQ.

Looking down at him, I thanked my God and my guardian angels for sending me such a creature to protect me from harm.

The Snake loved to fly. I never figured it out. He'd jump aboard an incoming bird and take it wherever it was going. Several days later, when he returned on another helicopter, I'd learn he had been with one or another of my advisory teams in the field. I'd hug him close and remind him he was needed here.

Most of our fighting occurred at night. We'd be informed by radio or most often by the noise of rifle fire and mortars from one sector or another. I'd call for a chopper and fly out to respond to the attack wherever it was. I always invited my counterpart, the district chief, to fly with me. Most often, my only companion was Snake.

One night, we flew over a hamlet getting hit hard. I called in mortar and artillery fire and adjusted it as best as I could in the dark. Our ship was taken under fire from the ground. Rounds came up through the belly of the Huey. One of them hit and smashed a flashlight sitting on the bench between The Snake and me. One of the shards must have hit my right temple because I felt blood running down the side of my face. I heard Snake squeal. I thought he was hit.

I felt for him in the dark. He jumped up and was licking at my face. He wasn't wounded but knew I had been hit.

The primary challenge to the defense of these highland hamlets from Communist incursion was the means of adequate communications. When a hamlet was overrun by VC or NVA, we often didn't know about it until days later when one of the citizens of the hamlet would come by the district HQ and tell us about it.

None of the villages or hamlets had telephones, and most of them had no radios. What radios they had were the older Korean War vintage PRC-10 type, FM tactical radio. Its range in the jungle rarely exceeded ten yards. The Communists pretty well had the run of the district, and we couldn't do anything about it without timely notification.

During my first tour in Vietnam, our combat units had traded out the PRC-10 for the newly developed PRC-25. The impact that radio made was immediate and phenomenal. We stretched our radio range from almost nothing in the jungle to nearly twenty-five miles under any conditions of terrain or weather.

Successful counter-insurgency operations followed the old Army adage: "If you ain't got commo, you ain't got nothin.'"

I knew that somehow I had to get my hands on some PRC-25 radios. I met with a fire support coordinator from the American Fourth Infantry Division elements located within our district who promised he could get us some radios. I told him we needed at least fifty of them. He blanched at the number but said he might be able to get that many if the division had some say as to where they would be located. I set up a meeting with Major Tan, our regional communications advisor, the fourth division fire support coordinator, and me to determine the best places to locate the radios. We selected the most trusted hamlets, ensuring as much as possible that the radios would not fall into Communist hands.

When I was assured we would get the fifty radios, I held a full-day's meeting at with the village chiefs of the selected villages and the people who would operate their radios. We knew that if a village was being overrun, anyone found operating a radio would be killed along with his family, so my message was simple. With Major Tan to interpret the instructions and Snake standing by to make sure all were paying attention, I said, "If you are attacked, call district headquarters, change frequency, and hide the radio. I will hear you and come with many guns."

I repeated that message again and again during training sessions on the use and maintenance of the new radios. We needed the Montagnards to have confidence in our ability to respond to their calls for help.

We didn't have long to wait for the results of our planning. The first night after training was over, we got a radio call from Pleikleng, the southernmost of our villages, hard by the border with Plei Ku province, that they were under attack.

I called Kon Tum and requested a helicopter for immediate pick up at Kon Tum. Next, I called for preplanned artillery fire.

Then I called in a request for immediate Air Force support to drop flares of the village so we could see what was happening.

This accomplished, I called in to regional operations in Kon Tum City, gave them a situation report, and requested that they relay that report to Plei Ku and all units operating in the Pleikleng area.

"Tell them it's about to get very noisy in that area."

Finally, I called Major Tan and invited him to join me at the helipad.

I grabbed my flight helmet, flak vest, and M16 rifle. I turned to Snake who had been watching me from his chair. His ears perked as he heard the approaching Huey.

"C'mon, boy, we got work."

We sprinted in the dark together, the small black dog and I, to the helipad where we were joined by my counterpart, Major Tan. The chopper settled, and we climbed aboard.

I spread my flak vest on the canvas seat and sat on it. Snake joined me, and Major Tan sat beyond us in the dark.

We pulled pitch and rose into the darkening sky. I briefed the pilot. The Snake sat silently beside me. To his right sat Major Tan. I checked to see the major was properly belted in. He said nothing. He crouched against the bulkhead wearing his flak jacket like a Linus blanket. I got the feeling he would rather have not participated in the evening's events.

The wind screamed through the open doors. The mountain air was cold. The gunners occupied their normal places on each side of the ship, alert to any movement that would cause them to respond with M60 machine gun fire.

Snake crouched close at my side, not afraid but very alert, the red instrument lights reflecting in his black eyes. I hugged him close.

I checked my map carefully by red light when we approached the besieged village. Smokey dropped flares that lit up the village. Snake drew closer as we felt the concussion of 155 howitzer shells.

After some minutes of sustained artillery fire all around the village with illumination fired directly overhead, I called cease fire and went down to take a close look. I saw no movement or signs of fighting on the ground. Beside me, The Snake was sleeping soundly.

I leaned toward Major Tan. Shouting over the noise of the chopper engine, I said, "Thieu-Ta, I don't see anything happening below. I suspect our new communications system is being tested. Please take my headset and see if you can get a situation report from Pleikleng." Keying my set, I said to the pilot, "Chief, I'm going off station for a few minutes. Grab a little altitude, and keep circling the village. Keep your airspeed up, and all eyes on the lookout."

"Roger that," he responded.

I changed frequencies and handed my helmet to Major Tan. He fired off a series of short questions in Vietnamese, after which, he was silent for a few minutes. Then he took off the helmet and handed it to me. "He say VC attack on west side of village. Nobody hurt. He say we can go home now."

I cancelled all the support missions and gave the signal to return to district HQ.

Over a cup of coffee, Snake dozing at my feet and the sun preparing to rise, Major Tan and I compared notes and concluded we had indeed been tested. "Thieu-Ta," I said, "I think we should go to Pleikleng this morning and congratulate the people for the great job they did resisting the Viet Cong. I think there were no attackers. I think they were testing the truth of what we told them we would do in the event they sustained an attack. We undoubtedly passed the test. There may be more tests from other hamlets before the people come to believe in us. I intend to respond to every call. Do you agree?"

"Yes, Thieu-Ta Dixon. I agree this is the wisest course. We will drive together to Pleikleng, and I will give the village chief an award. Will you bring your medic in case there are any casualties?"

I nodded.

The Snake stirred and chuffed his approval of our plan.

From that time on for the remainder of my year's tour of duty in Kon Tum, The Snake and I flew together almost nightly in response to radio calls from villages. Sometimes, we responded to nothing more than a cricket's farting. More often, it was a bloody attack with rifle fire and grenades to which I responded with artillery and air strikes. As I promised, I spent a lot of time overhead in a Huey, adjusting fire and later bringing in dust off to evacuate wounded.

The Snake sometimes flew without me. He'd hop aboard a resupply chopper that landed on our pad and fly out to one or another of our remote advisory stations and spend a few days with the MAT (mobile advisory team) until he'd hop on another bird and return home to Kon Tum. The aviators thought he brought good luck and usually welcomed him aboard. I missed him when he was gone.

Through the ability to communicate, we had been able to change our status from reactive to proactive, and Charley got the word big time. His attacks fell off sharply.

Success produced more radios; we were able to supply communications to all 110 hamlets as well as the 56 larger villages. A Huey was on permanent standby for me. As the populace grew to trust in our immediate and lethal response to their calls for assistance, they became more and more resistant to VC and NVA (North Vietnamese Army) incursions.

We heard small arms and automatic weapons fire from the north of our team headquarters. We discussed its location. A call came in from the village of Tri Dao, about a mile to our north. The report was, "Many VC attacking from the north side of our village."

I called for my chopper, and as it settled on the Kon Tum District pad, Snake and I hopped aboard and took our usual position; I was behind the pilot who sat in the left front seat. The dog sat beside me on the canvas bench. I sat on my flak jacket and shared as much of it as I could with Snake.

I plugged my helmet into the intercom system and said, "And with whom do I have the pleasure of sharing tonight's adventure?"

"Chief Warrant Officer Lewis, sir."

His voice sounded very young and very scared.

"Welcome to Kon Tum, Chief. Your first combat mission?"

"Yes, sir."

"You do know how to fly a helicopter, right?"

"Roger that, sir."

"Where'd you go to flight school?"

"Fort Rucker, Alabama, sir."

"That's great, Chief. You couldn't have gone to a better school. Now you just keep the bird in the air and follow my instructions. Snake and I will be your tour guide for the evening."

"Snake?"

"My dog."

"Sorry, sir. Dogs aren't allowed on board."

"Oh yeah? How many hours of flight time you got, Chief?"

"Five hundred."

"Well, this dog has more air time than you do. He stays. And don't act so scared. It makes the dog nervous. Oh, and don't call me 'sir' on the radio. It makes me nervous. On the air, I'm known as 'Whiskey Six.'"

"Our target area is a village about a mile due north of here. There'll be a lot of friendly artillery fire going in around the village and some Air Force fast movers in the area, so watch your altitude, and keep your air speed up. Keep close contact at all times with the FAC (forward air controller). Expect enemy ground fire. If we take a hit from an RPG (rocket propelled grenade), I expect you to get us home. You got it?"

"R-roger."

"Let's go."

We pulled pitch and circled tightly to the North. I warned the door gunners to expect a lot of heat. The gunners, old hands, licked their lips with anticipation. I noticed Snake did the same. He sat up and looked at me expectantly.

We approached the village. I anticipated RPG rifle fire and hand grenade explosions. I was not disappointed. We heard the sounds and saw the flashes as we flew over the target area.

I saw the village was getting hit hard. I called for artillery and air support. I knew there were many children in harm's way.

"We're way too high, Chief. I can't see anything."

"Roger."

He began to cut his air speed.

We descended and entered an area close enough to the target village that I could see where the enemy fire was coming from. I called the Air Force FAC and requested heat on the north side of the village.

"Roger that, Whiskey Six. I have napalm on call. Will deliver as requested."

I was always nervous about napalm. I gave my full attention to making sure the fires were on target.

My pilot flew low and slow over the village. I became aware of that when we began taking automatic fire up through the belly of the chopper.

The bird shuddered and began settling into the trees. I prayed to my guardian angels for help. We neared the ground. Snake jumped from the Huey and disappeared into the dark jungle below.

The helicopter dropped closer to the ground and then regained enough power to gain altitude as the young pilot fought for control. I remember praising his ability to gain control of the bird while worrying over what had happened to Snake. We were almost certain to crash in the jungle. If we survived a crash, we could face certain death at the hands of the enemy, probably NVA.

I don't remember much of that flight back to Kon Tum. I remembered skating above the tree tops. I remembered The Snake was gone.

I felt a sharp bump as the helicopter shuddered to a sliding stop on the tarmac.

"Great job, Chief. They taught you well at Fort Rucker. Door Gunners, you okay?"

"Number 1, okay."

"Number 2, okay."

"Right seat, okay?" There was only silence from the right seat.

The pilot said, in a voice shaky with fatigue, "He's unconscious. I think my copilot's been hit."

A fire truck and an ambulance careened up to the now completely dead helicopter. I jumped to the ground and directed the medics to the right door where they found the copilot bleeding from several bullet holes. He was dead.

The pilot dismounted and said, "W-w-what now, Major?"

"Whaddya mean, 'what now?' Go get another bird, and let's go. We gotta find the dog."

"Not me." The chief shook his head. "I've had it for tonight. Get yourself another pilot. I'm done."

The pilot walked away. I hurried to base ops to wangle another bird. By the time we were airborne, the sun was shining about the mountains. Kon Tum District called to request I stop and pick up Major Tan.

"Roger. Tell him to get to the pad, pronto."

We hurried out to district HQ, picked up Major Tan, and then sped to the village. Approaching the Tri Dao Bridge for landing, I looked about at the burning huts and people scurrying about like ants gathering the wounded in the village center. I called for dust off and reported our need for medivac. I scanned the ground but saw no sign of Snake. I didn't expect to see him—he'd be playing escape and evade amongst the Montagnard villagers who would kill and eat him if they could. Major Tan and I dismounted on the bridge and walked among the villagers, taking stock of wounded and killed. The village chief proudly displayed the bodies of several main line VC they had killed in the fight. I called for as many of my medics as I could muster to help with the wounded. Three of them arrived with the first dust-off bird and began rendering aid as fast as they could.

I called in a preliminary report to region. "We have seven local force soldiers KIA and seventeen villagers killed or wounded. One U.S. MIA, the team dog, Snake. There are seven Main Force Viet

Cong KIA. The enemy has been driven off to the north. Formal report to follow."

All in all, this counted as a victory. Our side had resisted for the first time and, for the first time, had caused the enemy to withdraw leaving his dead behind.

Colonel Whalen responded, "Whiskey Six, this is Champion Six—good work. The tables are turning. Keep me posted on the dog, out."

Major Tan gave a speech, praising the villagers for successfully resisting communist efforts to overrun the village while the medics treated the wounded and evacuated those who survived to the Montagnard hospital in Kon Tum City. The village elders collected the dead.

As the day ended, Major Tan and I retreated to the chopper for the return to district base. I stood on the skids and donned my flight helmet as the district chief mounted on the opposite side. I glanced in his direction and found The Snake sprawled sound asleep on the canvas bench.

As we pulled pitch and rose in the sky, I called in a report to province.

"Champion Six, this is Whiskey Six. The Snake has returned. I say again, The Snake has returned, over."

"This is Champion Six. Good work. I expect a full verbal report of action at our next briefing. I also expect you will bring the dog, out."

The village had been hit hard and survived what we learned later was a main unit of North Vietnamese Regulars. For the first time since I arrived in country, a small group of Popular Force village defense militia had beaten off what was later identified as a company of the 308th Division, North Vietnamese Army, Communist heroes of the French Indochinese War. We had begun to win. In this small corner of the Central Highlands, we had begun to drive the Communists back. I was elated that my strategy had been successful. Communications plus fire support had been the key. We were winning in Kon Tum District! It may have seemed small potatoes to the overall war, but to us, it was the difference between victory and defeat. It meant the people of South Vietnam had a chance to retain their freedom.

Altogether, Snake and I flew more than two hundred night missions against the Communists. We had two more birds shot out from under us, but neither of us sustained injuries beyond scratches, bruises, and sore muscles.

The following Sunday, Snake sat upright in the right seat of a jeep as I maneuvered the sandy track to Kon Tum City for the weekly briefing. We took my usual seat in the front row of the theater, The Snake next to me forcing the usual occupant to seek a seat elsewhere.

When Colonel Whalen called me forward to render my weekly report, he remained standing at the podium as I walked up accompanied by the dog.

"Attention to orders." All the men stood at attention as did I. Snake stood beside me, ears erect as the colonel announced, "Headquarters Department of the Army, Special Orders number 69-23 dated 29April1969, the dog, a member of the Kon Tum District Advisory Team, known as Snake, is awarded the United States Air Medal for service in the air under combat conditions."

The colonel placed the medal, attached to a ribbon, about Snake's neck. The dog stood taller, if possible, and looked out over the gathering of officers and enlisted men.

The men applauded and applauded again when I rendered my report of action at Tri Dao. I keep that air medal pinned to a picture of Snake and mounted on my bedroom wall to this day.

4

The Snake was not feeling well. His nose was warm; he began to suffer from mange and was generally listless. When this condition persisted and worsened over several days, I asked Dr. Pat Smith at the Montagnard hospital in Kon Tum if she could do anything for him. She agreed to examine the dog.

"But," she said, "I can't promise a diagnosis. Dogs are not my specialty."

After looking the dog over and poking him here and there, she said, "Well, he is surely sick, but with what, I don't know. Maybe he's been poisoned, but I don't know for sure. Can you take him to Plei Ku? The Army has a veterinarian there."

"A vet in Plei Ku?"

"Yes, his primary duty is inspecting meat and produce destined for military units. Maybe he can help the dog."

I travelled with Snake by Huey the fifty miles south to this largest of Central Highland villages where I found the vet residing at the Special Forces Compound there.

"You'll have to leave the dog with me until I've had time to examine him thoroughly. I'm very busy right now with a shipment of freshly slaughtered turkeys that's come in for Thanksgiving dinner. Call me in three days."

I flew home to Kon Tum alone and concerned. The vet seemed more interested in dead meat than live animals. I was worried the dog might end up on some mess sergeant's menu.

I went out on night helicopter patrol responding to calls for help for the next few nights alone. Without Snake, I felt somehow vulnerable, like I'd forgotten my sidearm.

I called Plei Ku by landline on the third morning and was connected to the vet.

"Captain Spheringen here."

"Hey, Doc, Major Dixon here. How's my dog?"

"Your dog's dying. I'm going to castrate him this morning. It's the only way to save his life."

Castration. I was shocked. How could that possibly be his problem?

"It's up to you, Major," he said as if reading my mind. "But if I don't operate now, he'll be dead by sundown."

I couldn't speak. The vet's attitude was like, "You want chops, or should I grind it into hamburger?"

Finally, I could speak. "Doc, you're not talking about just any Vietnamese cur here. Snake is a decorated hero. Operate if you think it will save him, but understand, if he dies, you'll answer to the entire Kon Tum region officer corps."

"I understand, Major." The vet was suddenly less sure of himself. "I'll do my best. Call me this evening."

I worried all day, attending to duties with difficulty. I called Plei Ku near sundown.

"Your dog is fine. You can pick him up any time after tomorrow."

The team rejoiced when I told them the news.

"It'll be good to have that mutt back," Burke said. "I haven't felt safe since he left."

"We gotta have a party when he gets back." Sergeant Pelky, our heavy weapons advisor, clapped his hands. "I'll lay on some steaks."

"We need some beer," somebody said.

"No. No beer here. Too dangerous."

I flew to Plei Ku the next morning and was shown to a row of cages, one of which held The Snake. He stood in his cage looking at me as if he was thinking, "How could you have done this to me."

"C'mon, boy, let's go home."

He jumped down when his cage door was opened and pranced at my side as we left the kennels. I looked down. He appeared to be his old self. When he spotted the chopper on the pad, he sprinted to spring up and into the interior. When I mounted and sat on the canvas bench, he rushed over and licked my face, something he had never done before. Then he sat proudly beside me for the ride to Kon Tum and home.

The chopper had barely touched down when he jumped out and ran for the team house and all nine of the advisory team who had turned out to welcome him home. He hopped up onto his chair and was there to smile and look at me when I entered the house.

That evening, we held a celebration for the return of Snake to active duty.

Snake's missing jewels didn't slow him down in his pursuit of Viet Cong. He was his old self now in ferocious pursuit of our enemies and just as MacArthur like in his mien among our ranks. He stood aside only for me and for Colonel Whalen, whom he somehow recognized as the big boss. He merely tolerated Colonel Duan, the province chief, and Major Tan, the district chief.

My time was growing short. SFC Burke wasn't a short-timer. He was next. I talked with him about taking The Snake home with me when my turn came.

"Don't think that'd be a good idea, Major."

"Why?"

"Snake belongs here. Takin' him out of the jungle would be like takin' one of us out of the Army. Besides, the team depends on him. He'd never make it stateside. Ain't sure I can either."

"Maybe you're right, Top Sergeant. I'll give it some thought."

Sergeant Burke rotated, and I hated to see him go. He was a combat soldier. I could not envision him fitting in to a stateside unit with its spit and polish. I knew he was right about The Snake.

A month or two after Snake's medical procedure, we discovered a local Vietnamese dog seeking refuge in a culvert running under our team compound. The local dogs looked like what I pictured African dogs looked like: light brown, short-haired, with long legs, between thirty and forty pounds. These dogs shied away from Americans; why, I don't know. Anyway, this dog was hiding in the culvert under our team house.

Sergeant First Class Crawford, our new team sergeant, came to me one night as I was filling out my progress reports.

"Sir, I think you'll want to see this."

I followed him outside the wire to the front of the American compound to the mouth of the culvert where he stopped and shined his flashlight into the opening. There, cuddled close to its Vietnamese mother, I saw a small black puppy.

Since Snake was the only black dog I had seen anywhere in the area and this pup appeared a miniature image of him, I could only conclude that Snake had sired him. How, I didn't know.

I had made friends with her, probably the only human friend she had ever had. I made her feel comfortable around Americans and thus drew her close to us. Apparently, Snake had got close to her. How he sired a pup after his neutering remained a mystery.

I knelt down before the culvert and retrieved the small, black puppy and took him into the compound. Snake welcomed him as his own. Though the bitch was not allowed inside our compound, she returned each night to lure the pup outside to hunt.

When I tried to discourage these nightly excursions, Snake apparently took my displeasure as a condemnation of the pup, so he drove the pup away, and we never saw it again.

Major Tan told me a tiger was terrorizing one of his hamlets. According to his reports, a tiger was entering the hamlet on a nightly basis and taking victims at will.

The people were frightened. Several pigs had been taken. No people thus far had become victims of the marauding tiger, but the people were terrified and calling on the government to remove this fearsome creature.

"Thieu-Ta, we must do something to help the people," Major Tan said. "You must go and hunt this tiger."

"Me?"

"I cannot go because of my crippled foot."

Major Tan had been wounded some years earlier and walked with a cane. Beyond that, I knew he was no combat soldier. It was left up to me to hunt down this beast.

"Who do you have who can track this animal?"

"Sergeant Truong."

Sergeant Truong was the so-called security sergeant for the district. He was not only a former member of the French Foreign

Legion, but also he was the chief assassin for the district. Several times I had noted, he had guided village chiefs on hunts and returned alone. I liked him, but I didn't trust him.

When I briefed my deputy advisor, Captain Rick Nelson, he became agitated and warned me not to do this.

"If you feel you must go, then I want to go with you."

"No. Somebody has to stay and run this show. That's you, Captain. I'll go and take The Snake to protect me."

"The Snake is no protection against tigers, is he?"

"He's the best protection I can think of. We don't know how he'll react to a tiger, but I'm willing to bet he'll give it his all. Besides, he will tip me off if Sergeant Truong turns against me."

I needed a weapon I could depend on in the jungle. My M16 was powerful enough to kill a man, but its rounds were easily deflected by foliage. I opted for a captured Czechoslovakian SKS rifle to provide the penetration I needed. My best weapon against a communist assassin, if it came to that, was The Snake.

"Thieu Ta, you give me claymore mines?" Sergeant Truong approached me on the day before we were to leave.

"What use are claymores against a tiger?"

"Not for tiger—for VC. We put them out to protect us when we sleep."

Against my better judgment, I gave him two of the mines, the deadliest weapon we had.

"You know how to use these?"

Truong nodded his head. "Pull safety pin here." He pointed to the back of the mine. "Place rods in ground, curved surface of claymore toward enemy." He pointed to the outside of the arced mine. Set trip wires here and here.

"Okay. Good. Use them wisely, my friend."

We started out late one afternoon. Sergeant Truong led. I followed. Snake stayed close on my heels. I felt the excitement of the hunt. We moved north into enemy saturated territory. We walked for three days and nights, stopping only to eat C-rations and rest briefly. I shared my rations with Truong and Snake. Water was readily accessible. I made sure to use plenty of halizone tablets to purify the water.

Each time we stopped, Truong placed the claymore mines out to provide protection and early warning of an attack. I checked to make sure he was placing them business side away from us. Snake merely curled up and went to sleep. I found his complacency reassuring.

On the fourth day, the tiger appeared. One moment, there was nothing. The next moment, he was there and coming fast.

Truong threw himself to the side, missing the tiger's fangs by inches.

I brought up the iron sights of the SKS and drew a bead on the head of the oncoming tiger. I remember thinking how beautiful he was.

I pulled the trigger. Nothing happened. The rifle misfired. All I could see was tiger fangs coming straight for me.

Out of the corner of my eye, I saw Snake running forward, barking and snarling toward the tiger. The animal, several times the size of Snake, stopped. He looked confused. He snarled at Snake. The dog growled and sprang for the tiger's face. Seeming perplexed, the tiger backed, spitting and snarling at Snake. The dog was indomitable. He would not be turned back.

I attempted to clear the rifle for another shot.

The tiger was gone.

"We go quick," Truong said. "Tiger get away."

"Let him go, for Pete's sake, let him go."

My immediate thought was that Truong had somehow slipped a bad round in my rifle so I'd be killed by the tiger. My reaction was to turn his game against him; shoot him and claim it was an accident. My second thought was I couldn't prove, nor could I believe that he would do that, and so I could not kill him.

Snake provided the proof for me. He never reacted toward Sergeant Truong as he invariably did to the Viet Cong. That was proof enough for me that Truong was innocent.

My decision not to kill the sergeant prevented me from committing murder.

The tiger was never again seen in that village. I think The Snake was just too much for him. Once again, I owed my life to him.

The days passed slowly, each one pretty much like another. The nights were more exciting and full of action. The seasons did not really change in the highlands, except in winter, the weather was drier and it got colder at night. It was cold enough to sleep under a blanket. Since we rarely got the chance to sleep at night, we took to wearing field jackets.

One day, late in my yearlong tour, a resupply chopper, destined for one of my mobile advisory teams located deep in the jungle, landed on our district pad. I knew it didn't contain one of our local crews because it circled once, looking us over carefully before it landed.

I didn't pay much attention except to note The Snake heading for the pad. I knew he'd hop aboard and ride out to spend some quality time with one of the mobile advisory teams. I always felt uncomfortable when he was gone. Enemy activity was increasing.

I was busy with paperwork in my radio shack, and while the chopper seemed to be sitting on the pad for an inordinate amount of time, I chalked it up to an inexperienced crew, probably from Plei Ku.

A call came through on the radio.

"Whiskey, Whiskey, this is Choir Boy 58. We got a problem out here on your pad. Request assistance, over."

"Roger, on the way," I responded, and picking up my flight helmet, I headed for the district front gate and the pad.

I wondered what the problem could be. I looked at the pad, some hundred meters away. There were no visible signs of trouble and no sign of Snake. I sprinted to the Huey.

I immediately got the picture as I stood on one skid and looked into the cockpit. There was Snake, standing in the chopper, growling and showing his teeth. The crew chief was backed up against the console between the pilot and copilot. The Snake appeared about to render him a eunuch.

"What's the problem here?" I said as soon as I'd plugged my flight helmet into the Huey coms system.

"This crazy dog insists on riding with us," the pilot said. "We don't allow dogs on board. You gotta get him offa here now."

The door gunners looked like they were about to fall out of the bird; they were shaking so hard with laughter.

"Chief," I said, "how long you been in-country?"

"About two months, sir. I know my regulations."

"Well, let me tell you something about your regulations, boy. How many air medals have you earned?"

"Well, none, sir."

"This dog has more combat flying hours than your entire crew. What's more, he has been awarded the air medal. He can fly anywhere he pleases in this district. Do you understand me, Chief?"

"I understand you, Major." He began to pull pitch.

I looked down at The Snake. We'd been through the mill together. We understood each other. I jumped down from the Huey. He jumped down with me. Before the chopper could get airborne, Snake lifted his leg nonchalantly and relieved himself on its skid. I wished I could do the same, but the Huey was up and gone.

One day, late in my tour, Sergeant Franco came running up to the radio room where I was doing my daily hamlet evaluation reports.

"M-M-Major," he said breathlessly, "I just seen a tank pick up The Snake and head down the road toward Kon Tum."

I stopped what I was doing. "What do you mean 'pick up?'"

Franco stood and pointed toward the road. "I seen an M48 stop out front and a guy got out, picked up Snake, and remounted the turret of the tank. The dog left in the tank. I seen it."

I called Kon Tum Regional Headquarters. "Downtown ops, downtown operations, this is Whiskey Six, over."

"This is downtown net control, send it, over."

"This is Whiskey Six. Request you keep your eyes open for a column of tanks passing through and headed south. One of them has The Snake aboard, over."

"This is net control. Understand the Americans have taken your team dog?"

"This is Whiskey Six. That is correct. The tanks should be passing through Kon Tum very soon now. Out."

I initiated a search of the compound to make sure the dog was gone. He was nowhere to be found, not a rare finding in the case of Snake who tended to wander among our field teams.

A short time later, I received a landline call from Colonel Whalen. "I understand your dog has been kidnapped by American forces."

"Well, I wouldn't say 'kidnapped' exactly, but he was last seen riding away in an American tank, toward the American brigade positioned to the south of Kon Tum."

"I'm sending out a Huey for you to conduct an air search for the dog. We need to get him back."

I didn't understand the colonel's sense of urgency, but I was willing to go along with him.

I was ready when the Huey landed on our pad and took off with them toward Kon Tum.

"Chief," I spoke over the Internet. "We should fly directly toward Kon Tum and look for a column of tanks either approaching or heading south from the city."

"Roger that."

We flew at about five hundred feet altitude toward Kon Tum.

"I see four tanks," the pilot said, "leaving Kon Tum toward the south. What am I looking for?"

"Snake is being transported by one of the tanks. Just follow them home. Let me know if you spot the dog."

"Roger that."

The helicopter followed the column of tanks down the highway toward the American compound.

"Oh, I got him," the copilot said. "He's standing, apparently in command, on the turret of the second tank in line."

"Good. Land on the brigade pad."

"Roger."

I was met by a sergeant apparently controlling traffic on the pad. He saluted and asked me what my business was at the brigade. "This helicopter is not authorized to land on this pad."

"This is an American pad, am I right?"

"Yes, sir."

"This is an American helicopter, am I right?"

"Yes, sir."

"I've come to get my dog. He's arriving on one of your tanks."

"Dog, sir?"

"Yes, take me to your commander."

The sergeant escorted me to the command post like I was a foreign visitor. He reported to a lieutenant colonel who turned to shake hands with me. "Welcome, Major. What can I do for you?"

"Sir, I am Major Richard A. Dixon, senior advisor to the Kon Tum District in which you are presently bivouacked. One of your tanks has made off with my team dog. I came to retrieve him."

The colonel looked surprised. "This dog must be pretty important to you to bring you flying down here to get him."

"He's one of our most important team members, and I expect he's reported to my chopper. If you'll excuse me, sir, I'll be on my way."

I faced about and hurried back to the chopper where I found Snake waiting for me in the cockpit. I replaced my flight helmet and said, "Mission accomplished, chief. Take us home."

"Roger that." He pulled pitch and headed north to the district pad.

As my time in-country grew shorter, the old team rotated stateside, and new faces appeared on my helipad. I rethought my decision to take Snake home with me. I researched procedures for what it would take. I asked The Snake, "How would you like to go home with me, boy?"

The dog wagged his tail slowly and looked at me with those black, black eyes that seemed to say, "Hey, boss, I love you, and I wish I could be with you forever. But my place is here with the team."

He was right. I couldn't deprive the team of his wonderful heart and combat sense. I had to leave him in Kon Tum.

On the day I left Kon Tum, probably never to return, I gathered my gear and stood at the entrance to the team house, Snake at my side. I shook hands with all my troops. The Huey that would take me away came in and landed on the pad. I knelt to offer my goodbyes to The Snake.

He sat stiff and erect as I held him close in my arms. His eyes sparkled in the sunlight as I bent to look into them one last time. I wanted to remember him always as he was at this minute. I wanted him to know how much he meant to me. There are no words for what I felt at that moment. He appeared to understand as he licked my cheek in farewell.

The chopper pulled pitch and headed for Saigon and the Freedom Ship that would take me home. I turned back for one last sight of The Snake. I thought I saw him standing by the front gate of the compound, but I couldn't be sure.

Years later, when I was retired from active duty and living near Fort Lewis, Washington, I ran into Rick Nelson, my stalwart deputy from Kon Tum. We shared lunch at the officer's club and stories of the war in Kon Tum.

Over coffee, I asked him, "Whatever happened to The Snake? Do you know?"

"After you left, we received orders to reoccupy an abandoned village on the edge of the pacified area. Quang Tri—you remember it. You refused to send a team out there because you said it couldn't be defended and was out of artillery range. Regional HQ threatened to relieve you, but you stuck to your guns, and in the end, Colonel Whalen backed you. Remember?"

"Yes, I remember they wanted me to send an advisory team into the jaws of death."

"Right. After you'd rotated stateside and the colonel had also gone, regional headquarters relooked the situation. They ordered our new leader to send a MAT to accompany a regional force company to reclaim the village for the South Vietnamese Government."

Rick looked down at his coffee cup.

"Snake went with the MAT. None of them came back alive. We found the advisors' bodies. I personally searched the battlefield for the dog but never found him. I believe he died defending our team."

The battle in question occurred in 1969. As I write this story in 2017, by my calculations, The Snake died some forty-eight years ago, yet his soul fills my consciousness to this day. I keep his picture on my wall with the air medal awarded to him. His spirit will live in my heart always.

5

My family accompanied me to Fort Lewis, Washington, my next assignment after my second combat assignment in Vietnam. Headquarters Department of the Army assured me that I would have at least two years at home before facing a third tour in the Nam.

I settled in with my family on the fort as comfortably as I could. Two years in combat changes a person, and I had trouble adjusting to garrison life. I had spent my teen and college years camping, fishing, hiking, and climbing in the Cascade and Olympic Mountains. Now I wanted to share that experience with my family. Unknown to myself at the time, I was searching for redemption from the guilt I felt as every soldier feels after taking life on the battlefield. I didn't understand my feelings until I began my writing career and experienced the catharsis of forgiveness as I wrote about the war.

It felt good to be home with Brenda and the kids. Cindy was in fifth grade now. Evelyn was in the first grade with Chris, though she was a year older. She had repeated kindergarten. I thought her being kept back might have been caused by my going away "to the war."

I took the family camping as much as I could. I wanted them to learn to appreciate the experiences of my youth. I bought a pickup truck with a canopy over the bed and built a bench in the back for the kids that would fold down into a sleeping platform for Mom and Dad when out camping. A typical camping trip to the Olympic National Park would find Brenda and me sleeping on air mattresses in the back of the truck, Evelyn and Chris sharing a pup tent, and Cindy reclining in my VC hammock under a tree. As often as not, we'd be camping in the rain.

One afternoon, in the spring of 1970, I was steelhead fishing alone on the banks of the Nisqually River. I seldom caught any fish, but when I did, the fight of this sea run rainbow trout, averaging ten pounds in weight, was worth the effort. They tasted good too.

I spent a restful two hours fishing the river and came away without a strike, but it was okay—I felt at peace as I broke down my fishing rig and stored it in the back of my truck.

I felt eyes on me. A flashback and I was once again in the jungle. I looked about out of the corner of my eye, alert to possible attack. I caught movement from behind a salal bush. I thought at first it might be a coyote or a fox. I called out to the animal. It peeked out at me, and I saw it was a small dog or a puppy—no a wolf cub. A wolf cub? How could that be? I decided it was indeed a puppy but a very strange and wild-looking puppy. It looked to be two or three months old. Its ribs were showing, and it appeared to be starving. Its eyes were wild looking.

I called to the animal and knelt on the ground. I saw it was a male. "Here, boy. C'mon, pup. I won't hurt you." Pursing my lips, I made kissing noises.

The pup came hesitantly at first, approaching and then running back to cover. At last, he came close enough to smell my outstretched fingers. I continued to kneel, petting and stroking the dog. I spoke calming words as I checked him for wounds.

I looked around and tried to think, did I see any other fishermen to whom this dog might belong? I had seen no one.

I picked the pup up. He weighed a scant ten pounds, but by the size of his feet, he promised he'd grow to be a big dog. He had a black and tan coat and a tail that curled tightly over his rump, like a husky. He was freckled on his flanks and his face.

He didn't like being picked up and struggled against me. I opened the door of my pickup and dropped him on the seat. I saw blood spots and realized he'd bitten me on the hand. "Why you, you bummer. You surely are a bummer, aren't you?"

The dog shrank into the corner formed by the seat and the passenger door. He made no sound, just looked at me with those wild eyes. I realized there was no way I could let him go now. I needed to have him tested for rabies. I closed the driver's door from the outside, took out my handkerchief, and wrapped it around my hand as I stood studying the woods around the truck.

The river and its banks were vacant. I looked across at the Indian reservation and formulated a theory. This pup had strayed from the reservation and fallen or jumped into the river and came up on the military reservation side. He must have been wandering for days with nothing to eat.

I opened the truck door and sat behind the wheel watching the dog all the time. He was still backed up against the passenger door, baring his teeth at me. I thought about letting him go free but knew I couldn't now. I reached out to pet him, and he snapped at my hand.

"Ow. You really are a bummer, aren't you? That's what I'll call you—Bummer."

I attempted to sooth him. "That's a good boy. Be a good dog now." I started the engine and drove the several miles back to the officers' quarters on Fort Lewis.

I tried to formulate a plan. *How would my wife accept this half-wild puppy? She'd not had a dog since Little Joe. How would my children react to this puppy's wild ways? Would he calm down once he got acquainted with us?*

This dog must belong to someone. I'd have to make an effort before claiming him as my own, but first, I must take him to the vet.

I parked the truck in front of our quarters and sat studying the dog beside me. He looked up at me with intelligent eyes as if he was reading my mind. I reached out and stroked his coat. He jumped up and came to me as if to say, "Take me, I'm yours."

I'd have to turn this dog in to the post veterinarian. I'd have to advertise that I'd found a dog. The fact was here was a real dog—I wanted him for my own. The challenge was how could I sell him to Brenda.

I left the dog in the cab of the truck and went inside.

"Hi, babe." She was cooking supper. The kids were fighting in the living room. Brenda gave me a hug and a kiss. "Catch any fish?"

"Naw, but I caught something else."

"Oh. What?" She spotted my handkerchief wrapped hand and was startled.

"I found a dog, or he found me. He was running loose in the woods. I looked for his owner, but there was nobody. The poor little guy's hungry, so I brought him home."

"Where is he?"

"In the truck. I'll go get him."

I picked the pup up in my arms and took him into the house. He squirmed but not so much as he had before. I found out he was not accustomed to the interior of houses.

"Are you sure this is a dog?" Brenda said.

"Pour him some milk."

She did as I asked, and I placed the puppy on the floor. We watched him lap at the milk hungrily until it was gone. He licked the bowl dry and then stood looking at us as if to say, "Please, sir, I want some more."

Brenda, oh, she of the soft heart, poured some more milk into the bowl and cracked a couple of eggs into it. The dog lapped at it until it was nothing more than a memory. Then he set about exploring the house.

"Dick, this is a valuable dog. Somebody's probably looking for him now."

Just then the dog discovered the kids watching *Scooby-Doo* cartoons in the living room. We heard thumping and ran to discover the kids jumping up and down as the pup ran to each of them in turn.

"Daddy, Daddy," Evelyn screamed, "can we keep him?"

I looked at Brenda. She looked at me.

"I don't think so, kids. Somebody's missing this dog right now. They're probably crying because he's lost. We gotta try and find them tomorrow. For tonight, the dog will stay with us."

"Awww, gee, Daddy," Cindy said. "He's so cute. Why can't we keep him?"

Again, I looked at Brenda. "We'll see." Brenda looked skeptical.

Chris, who was five at the time, wrote his version of the event many years later.

The first time I saw Bummer, we were living at Fort Lewis. Dad had been fishing that day. He brought home what looked like a fuzzy, matted thing in the front seat of his pickup. It kept darting about and wouldn't sit still. I thought it was a wolf or a coyote. When Dad let it out, it ran around the truck, not playfully, but in a wild, lunging way. He was mostly black and tan with a tightly curling tail. Dad told me it was a puppy, but it was unlike any puppy I had ever seen. It seemed more like the stuff bad dreams are made of. I was scared of this wild animal. When Dad brought it into the house, it ran about frantically looking for a way out. When Mom gave the dog a bowl of bread and milk, it devoured the food in seconds as if it hadn't eaten for a long time. Mom gave it some more, and it gobbled it down too. It ran a few more laps upstairs and down, apparently looking for a way out, before it finally began to settle down. Mom and Dad seemed pleased with it. I couldn't fathom what they saw in it. It appeared to me like a wild and dangerous animal, unlike the cute little dog we had recently given away. He was a cute little guy who only gnawed on toys and furniture. This dog was more likely to chew on us. The next-door neighbors owned a yappy Scottish Terrier who considered himself the Alpha Dog of our neighborhood. He gave Bummer a few seconds tutelage until Bummer tired of the game and sent the Scotty packing. Time passed and I began to recognize Bummer for the truly fantastic animal he was. We bonded forever or his lifetime, whichever ended first. I found out Dad had placed signs around that we had found a lost dog. I was scared we might not get to keep him. Thankfully, no one answered those notices.

I checked with the post vet, put up posters in all the right places, posted a notice in the paper, and even visited the Indian reservation but was invited off before I could tell them why I was there.

Meanwhile, Bummer had taken over the house and the children. He watched over both with canine caring.

A month went by, and I took the dog to the vet for shots.

"What kind of dog do you think this is," I said.

"Dunno, he's pretty wild," the vet said. "I'd say he was about half malamute and half wolf. You sure you want to keep him?"

"All bets aren't in yet." I wanted him. The children adored him. I needed Brenda's input before I could say, "Okay, Bummer. You belong to us."

It was plain to us that this dog was aggressive and more than half wild. Though he identified with our family and let the children have their way with him, we had to be careful because post regulations were really tight on "pets" and their behavior. We were mindful of our experiences with Little Joe on Okinawa.

A few weeks later, I had the time to go fishing again. I decided to take Bummer with me.

"Do you think that's a good idea?" Brenda said. "He might run away from you. He might rejoin the Indians across the river."

"It'll be a good test. If he wants to go back, we're better off knowing now."

I drove down to my usual parking spot on the river. I watched the dog as I rigged my steelhead gear. He hopped out of the truck and began circling and smelling, checking for p-mail.

We walked up the riverbank together. I watched the water carefully for signs of fish and watching the dog closely to see what he would do. He ranged about, sniffing at everything, but stayed close to me. The river was still high, running fast and clear. It was good for steelhead fishing.

Arriving at my favorite fishing spot (steelheaders called it the Stove Hole, perhaps because a rusting coal range rested on a rocky ledge in the middle of the river), I bent my hook through a sticky glob of salmon eggs, attached a lead sinker, and cast it out into the river to drift down with the current. When I felt the sinker bouncing along the rocks at the bottom of the run, I knew I had just enough weight.

This was one of the few days left in the winter fishing season. The weather was clear and unseasonably warm. The sun was shining brightly as it always did on the few days this time of year when it showed itself at all.

The Bummer mounted a large boulder standing just downriver from where I stood. He stood sniffing the wind, looking for all the world like Yukon King. Then he sat down to watch me cast out into the swift running waters.

I worked the Stove Hole for maybe half an hour when I felt the slight hesitation of the bait that told me a stealie had picked it up. I set the hook, and a good-sized fish broke water right in front of me. I played him for a few minutes while Bummer stood on his rock watching the action and cheering me on with his barking. Then without warning, he launched himself off the rock and into the water.

My attention shifted from the steelhead to Bummer as he began to bob swiftly downward in the roiling river water.

Without hesitation, I dropped my fishing rod and sprinted downriver, underbrush slapping at my arms and face. If he could swim, I needed to be at the place where he came ashore. The banks were undercut along this area and might suck, what seemed at this moment, a small and very vulnerable animal down to his death. *All dogs swim, don't they? Please, Lord, let him make it to shore.* I struck onward through the brush trying to keep him in sight. The river seemed to laugh at me and jeer as it pulled the dog further toward the middle.

I tired. My breath grew labored. I hurried on, knowing there were rapids and a falls ahead. If he reached the rapids, he would not survive. It seems he read my mind because his efforts doubled and he managed to reach an eddy and a jam of broken logs. He struggled to climb over the flotsam.

Reaching out as far as I could, I managed to grasp a handful of hair at the nape of Bummer's neck and pull him up and over the logs to shore.

Gasping for air, I dropped to the ground, hugging the sodden dog to my chest. Bummer broke away and shook himself vigorously to dry himself and soak me. He stopped and licked my face, looking at me with an expression I was to learn was his way of laughing. He took this whole adventure as great good sport.

"Oh, Bummer, you little bugger. You really are a bummer, aren't you?" I hugged him tightly.

He looked at me, tongue lolling, and seemed to ask, "Aren't we having a grand adventure?"

I walked back up river, Bummer following, to retrieve my rod, rebate to hook, and cast into the stove hole once more. Bummer promptly mounted the rock and launched once again into the tumultuous river.

I watched him bob up and down with the current. "Okay, you Bummer you," I called after his small, receding body. "This time, you can make your own way back to shore."

I packed it in and began to walk back down the river, watching all the way for The Bummer to appear. When I reached the rapids, I looked carefully over every stretch of water for signs of the dog. When I was certain he wasn't there, at least not visible on the surface of the water, I continued downhearted to my truck. *Oh, my poor puppy. I should have reacted quicker. Now you're dead, and it's my fault. What am I gonna tell Brenda and the kids?*

I arrived at the truck to find Bummer sitting by the driver's door. When he saw me, he stood and shook the last of the river water from his pelt. At first, I was angry. "You dog. Where you been?" Then I knelt and hugged him close.

He looked into my eyes, licked my nose, and seemed to tell me, "I am a dog. Never try to make something else of me, and I will be loyal to you all my life."

He was a dog. He was my dog. I needed no more commitment from him. I understood that I had only to love him. No. He needed no commitment from me except I accept him as a dog. Nothing more, nothing less.

From that day on for the remainder of his life, Bummer and I were partners. He loved the family, and the family loved him. We all knew he was a special dog, not a pet, and we would have to accept and respect him as a dog.

I didn't realize until years later that I had been suffering from the effects of PTS, not PTSD, because I certainly wasn't disabled, but I suffered the same stress endured by all combat veterans. The medics hadn't put a name to it yet, but we all came home to different lives. We were changed by battle, and we looked at life in a changed way. Fishing was a way for me to cope with feelings of not belonging. My family dealt with it in different ways. Some families broke up, but mine didn't. When Bummer signed on, he helped us to meld together as a team. He helped me. Only now, years after that dog died, do I recognize that truth.

Throughout the following years in Washington, Alaska, and Minnesota, we were to spend many happy hours together, The Bummer and me, on one river or another.

There were times I regretted having a dog like this. He was always a little wild. Whenever we went camping, we didn't bother to bring dog food with us. Bummer preferred to live off the land. Living on Army posts, we had to be careful—Army regulations were strict about "pets." It seemed at times we were forced to make life decisions forced by the fact of The Bummer's existence. Looking back, I wouldn't have had it any other way.

6

I had come home from Vietnam to Fort Lewis for what was to be not more than a year or so, and then I expected to be sent back to the jungle. I figured I had used up more than nine lives and I wasn't even a feline. A third tour in the Nam might be final for me. I had a chance to build a house in Tacoma and took it. I'd need to prepare a permanent place for my family in case my luck ran out. Short months after The Bummer became a member of our family, we moved off post and into our own home surrounded by the forests of Western Washington.

Cindy started the seventh grade, and the two little ones, Evelyn and Chris, started first grade together. Each morning, when I left for work on the post, Brenda would relax at the kitchen table for a second cup of coffee and conversation with Bummer. She'd talk to him, and he'd answer with an assorted vocabulary of growls, squeals, and barks that she understood was his way of telling her he loved her.

We all settled into our new digs. It was comfortable, and we were happy, despite Brenda's and my anticipation of the arrival of overseas orders. The dog settled in and was content except for two irritations: mail carriers and cats.

Soon after we had moved in, I installed a cable in the front yard between two Douglas firs. To this cable, I hooked a leash for Bummer so he could range the yard almost unrestricted. Unfortunately, one end of the cable was near our mailbox.

One day, a few weeks later, I was home for lunch when the mail was delivered. I heard Bummer barking, and jumping up, I discovered the postman baiting Bummer. The dog was straining at his tether, teeth barred, trying to reach the postal carrier while the carrier taunted Bummer with a stick.

I ran out. "Hey, don't do that. What's the matter with you?"

The carrier hopped into his truck. "Ya oughta keep that animal caged," he snarled as he sped away.

Chris wrote: *Have a brief memory of an incident involving a mailman. Bummer was tied to a runner line strung between two trees in the front yard. We suspected the mailman taunted the dog whenever he delivered the mail. One day as he passed, Bummer pulled himself free of his chain and chased the mailman down the street. The mailman never parked in our driveway again.*

I hurried over to the dog. He sat before me, head bowed, ready for his punishment.

I kneeled before him and took him in my arms. I saw that he had been subjected to daily taunting during a time when we expected him to adjust to his new environment. I vowed never to chain him up again. I researched the county statutes and found there was no leash law in my area. I decided to let Bummer run loose and take my chances with the neighbors. The dog had proven himself to be a secretive creature that avoided human contact other than those of his own family. I believed he offered no threat to the neighborhood. I was proven wrong on only two occasions except that for the remainder of his life, Bummer couldn't abide mail delivery people. We continued to treat Bummer like an inside dog but gave him the run of the neighborhood. Mostly, he hung close, but sometimes, he would be gone overnight and show up the next morning covered with mud and hanging his head. We thought he must be in love, but later, I became convinced he was hunting down at the pond.

Chris wrote: *When we left Fort Lewis for our new home in Lakewood, a suburb of Tacoma, I had grown to really love our dog, Bummer. I had thought of him as a big dog when we got him, but now he seemed to have grown larger than life. Mom and Dad let him run free in Lakewood, and he often wandered down to the pond at the end of our street. I remember going down there many times to have him emerge from the bulrushes to greet me, tongue lolling and wanting to be petted before disappearing in the bushes, not to be seen again until time for chow. I remember once, when a neighbor's dogs came into our yard and ate from a bowl left out for Bummer. Bummer saw them and gave chase.*

The other dogs ran back to their yard, but instead of following them, he jumped over a high fence. I'm sure it wasn't all that tall, but it was much taller than I was. This seemed to me to be a feat of epic proportions. What happened next, I couldn't see through the fence, but the sounds were frightening. They made me very afraid. Moments later, Bummer returned, tongue hanging low and jaws covered with blood, not his own. I never saw those dogs again. Bummer earned the reputation among the canine crowd of a dog not to be messed with.

We lived close to the Army post, and I often came home for lunch. One day, I was sitting at the kitchen table eating a sandwich. Looking out the window, I noticed the neighbor's Siamese cat sunning him or herself on the split rail fence that separated our properties. I thought little of it but wondered where the dog was. As if he heard me, I saw him emerge from around the corner of the house. At that time, he was, I hoped, about half grown and weighed about thirty-five pounds. He was mostly a happy puppy. Now he pranced up to the fence, tail wagging and wanting to play. He'd never seen a cat before.

The cat sat up and spit at the dog. Bummer hesitated then barked and jumped, perhaps expecting the cat to run like the many squirrels and chipmunks he'd chased. The cat decided to take a ride and jumped on Bummer's back and, sinking his/her claws into the dog's shoulders, settled back for a ride.

Bummer, with cat aboard, disappeared rapidly down the street.

When he returned, sans cat, looking like there might have been a canary involved, I checked him all over for injuries. Finding none, I gave him a good rubdown.

"That's a boy. That's a good Bummer boy."

He looked up at me, tail erect and curled tightly, tongue lolling, wearing a satisfied smirk I was to learn was his way of proclaiming victory over an enemy.

I wondered about the cat. It appeared a few days later in its favored spot on the fence. I knew this was a valuable cat and our neighbor was a favored fishing buddy of mine, so I went next door to explain the cat was in danger sitting on the fence. They politely blew me off. I told Brenda to try and shoo the cat away if it appeared again on the fence.

A few days later, the cat was again sunning itself on the fence while I was home for lunch. I started up to go and chase him away, when I saw Bummer, not much more than a blur as he sped toward the fence and launched himself over the cat. I ran outside and found the cat, its back broken, laying at the foot of the fence. Bummer was nowhere to be seen.

I picked up the cat and carried it next door. The kids cried when they saw the dead cat. I wanted to say something like, "I told you so," but merely said, "I'm terribly sorry for your loss and will pay for a new cat."

The Bummer returned after dark that night. He was covered with mud. I knew he had been down at the local pond, hunting for frogs. I took him into the garage and hosed him down. Then I toweled him off and fed him a steak to let him know all was forgiven.

When, the next day, the neighbor presented me with a bill for five hundred dollars, I knew our days fishing together were over. "I'm sorry," I said. "I guess you'll have to sue me."

Nevertheless, I went down to the animal rescue center in Tacoma to see if I could find a replacement cat. They had a lot of feline inmates. I looked them over and selected one I thought resembled their cat.

When I rang their front doorbell, the wife answered, and when I presented the new cat, she looked at me, grabbed the cat, and slammed the door in my face.

On another occasion, our kids were playing in the street with the neighbors kids—yep, the ones with the cat.

When I returned from duty one evening, Brenda, with tears in her eyes, told me the kids had been playing together in the street. One of the neighbor's kids was a deaf child. She was used to getting her way because of her disability. She had apparently not liked something Evelyn had done and took a swing at her. An altercation between the two little girls followed. Bummer intervened, jumped between the two girls, and scratched the deaf girl's face.

"The next thing I knew," Brenda said, "Bob showed up at the front door brandishing a very large pistol. He was barely coherent, wanted to know where the dog was, and threatened to shoot him. I slammed the door in his face and made sure Bummer was in the house."

Chris wrote: *One day, while out playing with the kids next door, my sister Evelyn got into a scuffle with a little girl named Carrie. She was deaf and was a brat. She was spoiled by her parents on account of her handicap. She pushed Evelyn, and Bummer ran between them apparently to protect Evelyn from attack. He jumped up on Carrie and scratched her eyelid. She ran home crying. I believed Bummer was just trying to be a good shepherd.*

I called for The Bummer. He approached me bravely but crestfallen. He knew he'd done wrong. I knelt before him and stroked his coat. I called for Chris and Evelyn. They stood before me with tears in their eyes.

"Tell me what happened with the neighbor's little girl."

They both told me the story in their own words. I gathered the dog had acted to protect Evelyn. While hugging the stroking the dog, I told them that I always wanted the dog to protect our family from anyone who wanted to do one of us harm.

Then I went next door looking for Bob. I found him working on his Volkswagen in his garage.

"I understand my dog hurt your little girl today."

Bob stood, wiping his hands with a towel. I watched for any aggressive action. We were both combat veterans.

"That's right," was all he said.

"Is she okay?"

"Yeah, my wife put a Band-Aid on it."

"I understand you came over to my house with a pistol?"

"Yeah, I was a little upset."

"Well, Bob I gotta tell you, you and I have been good friends. But if you ever come armed to my house again, you'd better be prepared to use it because I will kill you."

It was the end of a friendship, and I had to decide whether my dog was worth losing a friend over. I thought long and hard about it. Finally, I decided that Bummer was family and worth more than anyone outside our family. Over the next few years, I often felt my freedom of action was restricted by the existence of Bummer in our lives. Each time I considered my options, The Bummer won out. He was worth makings sacrifices for.

During the first year of his adoption, we went camping whenever the opportunity arose. I don't think Brenda enjoyed it that much, but she was a great sport about it. I think the children enjoyed it, and I thought of it as education for them. I know Bummer loved every minute spent in the woods.

Often, we'd just head out into the woods to camp. We'd avoid an established campsite so as to avoid people, their kids, and their dogs. We'd rough camp or no camp at all, just out in the woods. We shared our family.

Whenever we were camping out, Bummer never needed to be fed. He hunted and feasted on ground squirrels, chipmunks, and voles as well as the occasional rabbit. On those occasions, I think he stayed with us less out of need but more because he saw us as members of his pack.

I didn't know it then because we as a family were just doing what seemed natural but, in fact, we were raising an indoor dog. When we were home, Bummer spent each night in the house and was free to come and go as he pleased through a doggie door I installed through the back door. Most often, he'd spend the mornings with Brenda, seeing the children off to school, sitting by her knee as she enjoyed a second cup of coffee. He talked to her with growls, howls, squeals, and many grins. Then he'd take a stroll around the block to make sure all was well in his world. Sometimes, he'd go down to the end of our cul-de-sac and beyond to the small lake and hunt frogs and such.

The neighbors apparently grew accustomed to his roaming about the neighborhood. The Mills family who lived just across and down from us said they felt reassured whenever they saw Bummer moving about. They learned to leave him to his wanderings. I learned of his many neighborhood adventures from the children and most often needed not interfere.

The kids were growing, and they also began roaming the neighborhood, playing with other children, and generally doing what happy kids do. Usually, The Bummer was with them, and since he showed a special liking for children, we didn't worry about them. The kids prevented any bad reports of Bummer's behavior from reaching home. He took care of them, and they took care of him.

The next year was 1970. Rotations to Vietnam began to slow down. We were winning or losing—I never knew which. Orders were not forthcoming, and I continued to enjoy learning to live in a family-oriented environment. I anticipated an alert at any time to orders back to the Nam.

The Bummer was learning some of the same lessons as I was. When he reached full adulthood at eighty-five pounds, he developed a protective mannerism toward the children. He was absolutely loyal to Brenda and me and would obey each of us on the instant. Sometimes, though, I wasn't to learn of this until much later, he took family justice into his own paws. The kids learned quickly not to cross The Bummer.

He acted often independently. He never barked like other dogs to warn of intruders. His bark was always a sign of his joy or his contentment. When he perceived a threat, to himself or any member of the family, his only warning would be a low growl, or not, followed by an attack.

This trait brought us our most dire worry—what would Bummer do and would we know about it.

We were always most concerned when strangers were around. A door-to-door salesman might be in danger. A neighbor who walked in unannounced might be attacked. We were willing to risk these mischances in exchange for the security offered by this half-wild animal. I had after all become accustomed to Snake's protection in the Nam.

When friends came to visit, we always made sure the dog was locked up in a bedroom. Whenever he was exposed to our friends, most often, he ignored them and went into another room to sleep. He had an uncanny way of knowing relatives were part of the family and treated them as one of us. That didn't mean they were safe from

Bummer's chastisement. Brenda and I knew we had on our hands a half-wild dog that resisted taming. We were always on the alert whenever others, especially children, were in the house.

All the family loved The Bummer, and he loved us. Whenever we watched TV together, he would cuddle up to one or more of us and talk to us in growls and whimpers as one or another of us rubbed his belly or tickled his ears.

Often, when we had begun to treat The Bummer like any other dog, he did something to remind us of his wild roots.

The next winter brought no overseas orders and a good steelhead season. I was on the river with Bummer as often as duty allowed. The dog loved being in the woods as much as I did. Whenever I was lucky enough to hook into a big sea-run trout, taking to the air, as steelhead usually did, Bummer would gleefully dive into the river and swim out to help me land the fish.

One day, late in the season, I took a friend of mine, Keith, down to the river. He'd spent several unproductive seasons fishing for steelhead. He'd never hooked one. I bragged I had been taught the art by an old Norwegian—he'd have better luck if he came with me.

I parked my truck in the usual spot near the mouth of the Nisqually River. From there, Keith, Bummer, and I hiked upriver. Bummer, as was his habit, ranged about in search of rodents. Keith followed me.

We walked upriver until we came to my Stove Hole. I walked back down to where I showed Keith he should fish.

I returned to my spot and began to cast. Bummer took up his favorite spot on the rock overlooking the pool.

I hooked a couple of steelies and lost them as the dog dove in at each hooking and interfered with my playing of one, as I recall, really big fish.

I heard Keith sing out in the distance, "Fish on." I dropped my rod and ran down the trail to help if I could. He played the fish, Bummer and I cheering him on. We hoped to join in a celebration of his first landing of this most elusive of game fish.

Working on his own, Keith landed his first-ever steelhead amid shouts and barks of joy as I netted the big trout for him. It would weigh in at around twelve pounds. I slapped him on the back and celebrated his catch with him. Then I walked back to my own spot, Bummer following.

Keith cut a bush and hung one of the branches through the gills of the steelhead, leaving it hanging to air-dry.

I resumed casting into the Stove Hole. I didn't notice Bummer's absence until I heard Keith yelling, "Get away from my fish, you #$%& dog."

I dropped my rod and galloped downstream.

I spied Keith, waving his arms and cursing. I guessed what had happened. The dog came running to my side. "What's wrong, Keith?" I yelled. I knew very well what was wrong.

"That dog of yours stole my fish. I'm going to kill him."

Keith chased the dog up the river. I could see Bummer running with a piece of fish in his mouth. He saw this as great good sport. I sympathized with Keith. It was after all his very first steelhead in seven years of trying. At the same time, I hoped he would not catch up to The Bummer. I wasn't certain what the dog would do.

Keith ran out of steam. The dog was nowhere to be seen. I was confident he would circle around and meet me at the truck.

"Hey, man." I worked to keep from laughing. "Just think. You caught your very first steelhead. Maybe the dog ate it, but now you can claim it was a trophy fish—maybe thirty or even forty pounds. Who can dispute your call. I'll swear it was at least twenty pounds."

"If I get my hands on that dog, he won't live another day."

"I hope you don't mean that, Keith. We're still friends after all. My dog only did what was natural for him. If you wanted to keep your fish, you shouldn't have hung it out where the dog could get it. You know I wouldn't let you hurt my dog even if you could."

Keith calmed down, and we walked back to the truck together. Sure enough, The Bummer was waiting. He circled warily until Keith settled in the front seat. Only then would he hop up into the bed and curl up to nap for the ride home.

While Keith and I remained fishing buddies, Bummer never forgot and never forgave Keith for his actions that day on the Nisqually River.

7

During the onset of winter, 1971, I was alerted for reassignment but not back to Vietnam. That war was slowing down. My orders were to report for duty at Fort Richardson, Alaska, in February 1972.

I rejoiced. Not only was I not going into battle again, but also I was taking my family to a fisherman's paradise—all that and skiing as well. Bummer would do well in Alaska.

We spent hours in front of the fireplace that winter, talking and planning for our great adventure to The Great Land. The kids were excited. They loved playing in the snow. Bummer was excited. Brenda was thankful I'd not be required to go back to war but apprehensive nonetheless. She envisioned life in an igloo. Bummer sensed that something momentous was about to occur.

We planned to buy a four-wheel drive, and I would take it up the Alcan Highway. I anticipated driving to Alaska in midwinter to be an exciting adventure. The family would fly in to Anchorage when I had established our quarters at Fort Richardson.

I began shopping for a suitable vehicle. I tested each of them along the Puyallup River over east of Tacoma. The only one I could not stick in the mud was the new Chevrolet Blazer. I bought it and prepared it for the trip.

Our family spent many hours planning the move.

"What about Bummer?" Evelyn said.

"I think I'll take him with me. He'll make good company on the trip. If there's a problem, he can keep me warm."

Bummer was sleeping by the fire. He raised his head. "Mrrumph," he said, approving the plan," and went back to sleep.

Later that night, after the kids had gone to bed, I shared an idea with Brenda. I had been mulling the thought over in my head for some days.

"I know it'll take the better part of ten days to drive to Alaska. It'll be cold. The weather's bound to be ferocious, but I'll have a brand new four-wheel drive vehicle, and I have plenty of experience driving on snow and ice. What would you think about my taking Chris along with me? It would be a great adventure for him. We've not gotten along well ever since I returned from Vietnam. It would be a great chance to bond. That's providing, of course, his teacher agrees he can spare the time out of school."

"I think that's a wonderful idea." She smiled in the flickering fireplace light.

Chris's teacher thought he would gain a great advantage on his education—better than any he could get remaining in class. My orders were published along with instructions about travelling the Alcan Highway as well as required supplies like extra gas and tires.

Chris, the dog, and I took several practice runs around the Olympic Peninsula. I decided to retrofit the back seat, so it ran from front to rear along the driver's side so the dog would have a more comfortable position and easier access to the rear hatch to answer the call of nature. Bummer's excitement grew as he anticipated the adventure along with Chris and me. I installed a block heater in the Chevrolet that could be plugged into electric power to keep the engine oil from congealing in severe cold. We made final plans around the fireplace that winter of 1971–1972. Chris faced the challenge enthusiastically, and we began to bond as father and son. Together, we built a bond on the trip that exists to this day.

The girls seemed a bit put off by being left out of the adventure. "I want to go too." Evelyn griped.

"You will, but somebody's got to help your mother pack and get ready for a grand airplane trip to Alaska. That's you and Cindy."

"Airplane? Oh, I like airplanes."

"You and Cindy and your mom will fly to Anchorage to join us guys when I have found a house for us to stay in."

"Can't Bummer go with us?"

"We need Bummer with us. He'll help keep Chris and me company on the long, lonely, and cold road through Canada." I tried to make the ground trip sound as unpleasing as possible. "If there's a problem in the snow, we'll depend on Bummer to keep us warm."

The dog raised his head at the sound of his name and chuffed and went back to sleep.

D-Day, H-Hour, we launched on a rainy February morning before dawn. I wanted to beat the morning rush through Tacoma and Seattle. I didn't realize the morning rush hours through Vancouver, British Columbia, were altogether as frenetic as those along highway I-5 in Western Washington.

The Blazer was loaded and filled with gas. I carried ten extra gallons on the roof in accordance with orders. Chris was at his appointed station in the passenger seat, wide-eyed and raring to go. The Bummer, grumpy at being aroused so early, jumped aboard the truck and promptly went back to sleep. Brenda was calling out her mental check list of things we might otherwise have forgotten. The girls were asleep in their beds.

I kissed Brenda goodbye. "So long, sweetheart. See you in Anchorage," I said in my very best Bogie accent. She laughed, kissed both Chris and me, and hugged The Bummer. We launched. If ever there was a wagon train well prepared for an arduous trip west, we were it.

We sped north through Tacoma, Seattle, and Bellingham, crossed the border, and were well along Canadian Highway 1 in British Columbia before daylight.

Now it was snowing heavily, though not sticking yet. Our planned destination for the day was Prince George, British Columbia, the jumping off point for Dawson Creek and Mile One of the Alcan Highway. It snowed all day.

Each time we'd stop for gas or to eat, Bummer would see that as a signal it was time to relieve himself. I checked carefully to make sure there were no people or animals close by, especially other dogs. I'd open the rear hatch and let the dog out to do his thing. If there were others about, I'd take Bummer out on a leash.

This procedure worked well most of the time. Bummer had achieved full growth in his second year at eighty-five pounds. Wearing his full winter coat, he was, in his primeval way, a glorious sight. He looked twice his size in his winter coat. His thick outer coater covered a thicker under coat, which could protect him in the coldest weather.

He wasn't particularly dangerous to strangers and usually avoided them when he could. His appearance, like that of a wild wolf, was generally intimidating. Usually, people were happy to give him a wide berth.

Animals, particularly dogs, were another story. When confronted by a strange dog—showing his or her stuff as dogs do, barking and snarling, pounding front feet, circling as dogs do—Bummer would, without warning, go for the jugular and the kill. Most times, other dogs would retreat quickly and successfully. But for this reason, that Bummer was not like other dogs, I was always cautious with him. I tried to understand him at first and later to accept him for what he was—there was a wildness in him I could never understand.

When we reached Prince George in northern British Columbia, the snow was coming down harder. Looked to me like a blizzard was building, so I filled up with gas and pressed on up to the pass through which we must go to reach Dawson Creek. I didn't want to get stuck for more than a day in Prince George.

The road up to the pass was either paved or well-plowed snow. We climbed for an hour. The snow changed from large fluffy flakes to the smaller variety combined with wind that usually meant colder air and accumulation on the ground.

"Well, boys, if I didn't know better, I'd say we were in the middle of a blizzard."

Chris nodded his head and looked at me with the confidence only a son can have in his dad.

Bummer responded, "Mrrrfff," and stirred on his seat before going back to sleep.

We pushed to the summit in four-wheel drive with a strong following wind. We saw no traffic at all, not even a snowplow along the way.

"Looks like a late lunch today."

"That's okay, Daddy, 'cause we're tough guys. We can wait, can't we?"

I saw a new growth in the boy. We reached the pass, and I stopped to let the dog out to relieve himself. He did so and frolicked in the deepening snow. I was worried. We had seen no traffic all the way up, and the snow was about a foot deep on the road. I stood beside the silent Blazer and looked off into the snow driven valley. I hoped I'd done the right thing. Should I have brought my son into this desolation? Only the high-spirited dog gave me the courage to go on. I called to The Bummer. Out of the mist of the falling snow he came, so happy, so rejoicing in the winter weather; I could only share with him the exhilaration of it all. I knelt and hugged him close. I felt the fullness of his joy at living in his body. I wasn't afraid any more. His confidence leant me courage.

"Chris, come out and see this sight. I've never seen anything like it." The wind howled in the darkening sky behind us, blowing snow into the valley before us. We looked down into the valley below, the sun shone over all we could see. I had never seen the like of it. I pointed toward the valley with one hand on Chris's shoulder.

"Can you see off there? That's Dawson Creek. It must be cold and clear in the valley. We're looking at it through a veil of flying snow. What d'ya think?"

"Beautiful, Daddy."

The Bummer did his business and poked his nose here and there in the snowbanks looking for a possible vole. I called him back to the Blazer. We loaded up and headed downhill. The wind was so strong, we coasted into the nearest town about 110 miles away and hardly used a gallon of gas. The temperature must have dropped more than forty degrees as we descended.

We stopped in a small village for lunch. It was still snowing but not blowing so hard now. I let the dog out to do his thing. Then Chris and I stepped into the warmth of the café for lunch. The place was about half full of customers, maybe six or seven people.

"What place is this?" I asked the man behind the counter. There were good smells coming from the kitchen.

"Glad to see you, pardner. That's one fine husky you got there. Bet he's liking this snow. This is called Chestwynd. Would you sell that dog? Say, you didn't just come through the pass from Prince George, did you?"

"Yes, we did, and no, I won't sell the dog. Why?"

"That road has been closed for the last three hours. I can't believe you made it through. What's it like up there?"

I looked at Chris. He looked at me with a half smile and a look that said we'd done something nobody else could do.

"We got a good vehicle. I didn't know it was closed, whatever that means. Lots of snow blowing hard. Couldn't see much. If I was headed south, I wouldn't chance it now."

I learned that it was customary among travelers in the north to share information on road conditions where you came from.

We learned that the road on to Dawson Creek was hard packed snow and that it had stopped snowing there.

"You got the specialty of the house coming. Did you see any cars or trucks in the pass?"

"We didn't see anything or anybody. How far to Dawson Creek?"

"About sixty miles. Your boy got a good appetite?"

"He can eat whatever you bring him."

Chris put away a one-pound burger with all the trimmings. I managed a quarter pounder with all the trimmings.

A man dressed in trapper's clothes entered as we were enjoying pumpkin pie for desert.

"Say, Mister," he said. "That your rig?"

"Yes, it is."

"Right skookum rig it is, but I gotta tell ya, you'll lose them mud flaps the first cold snap we have. How much does that dog weigh?"

"About eighty-five pounds." I grew cautious now.

"Looks a lot heavier. Would you sell him?"

"I don't think so, but I'll have to ask his brother." I turned to Chris. "What do you think, son? Shall we sell Bummer?"

Chris was just finishing his pie. He looked up at me and then at the man. He stood with hands on hips and said, "No, sir. Not for a million scillion dollars. Daddy, can we go now?"

We hit the road for Dawson Creek. The weather had cleared, though looking in the rearview mirror, I could see the blizzard that still blew behind us. We arrived at Dawson Creek in sunshine and relatively warm weather. I recall it was about thirty degrees Fahrenheit. We pulled into the first motel I saw. It had a sleeping bear on its sign and an inviting restaurant. I pulled into the office and cleared Bummer for staying with us in a room with two double beds. As we pulled up to a parking place, I noticed it contained plug-ins for engine heaters, the first I'd seen on the highway north of Seattle.

We settled in. Chris noted there were two beds and his bed was as big as mine. Bummer circled the room. I was comforted that he refrained from lifting a leg.

Chris and I, leaving Bummer in the room, walked across the parking lot to the café. The country was flat with little timber anywhere in sight. There was little traffic in any direction. I noted a sharp sting in the air. The sun had appeared and was shining weakly. The temperature dropped.

The café was a clean, well-lighted place, with a good menu. The waitress was friendly. We ordered steaks, baked potatoes, and lemon meringue pie. I asked about road conditions to the north.

"Well, we've had a lot of snow, but the weather's been unseasonably warm, the plow's been working the road. It's a straight shot to Fort St. John. You should have no trouble."

"It seems to be getting colder. Do you think I should plug in my vehicle tonight?"

"Nope. It never gets cold enough this time of year. You can trust me."

Luckily, I didn't.

We left the café after a fine supper of pork chops and eggs. I felt my nostrils stinging in the afternoon air. The sun was setting rapidly in the west, and it was noticeably colder.

"Son, we better let Bummer out to do his thing and then turn in. We got a lot of miles to do tomorrow."

Chris agreed.

We went to our motel room and let the dog out to do his thing. As far as I could tell, we were lone boarders that night. We walked on top of a thick snow crust in the back of the motel. The breaths of us three were steaming. It hurt to breathe. The Bummer squatted to do his thing. He worked at it, yelped, and jumped. He repeated this several times before I realized he was reacting to cold air on his distended anus. He couldn't defecate.

"That's it, son. We gotta plug the Chevy in tonight."

8

We enjoyed a good night's sleep after our long drive the previous day. We had made it to Mile One of the Alcan Highway without incident, despite bad weather. The Blazer was performing well.

In the morning, I turned the television on to learn that last night's temperature had reached a record -47° Fahrenheit.

"Wow, Daddy. That's cold."

"You bet your boots it was. Let's hope the Chevy starts okay this morning."

We dressed and took the dog out to see if he could relieve himself. The weather was overcast and had warmed only slightly. Bummer ran across the parking lot and squatted to do his thing. He yelped a couple of times and managed to go. He looked for a place to dive nose first into the snow and hunt for vole, but the crust was too thick.

I inserted the key in the truck door lock, remembering too late that door locks might freeze up in the cold. Luckily, it worked smoothly, and I placed the key in the ignition and twisted it. To my relief, the engine turned over immediately. I left the engine running and unplugged the vehicle from the post.

We put Bummer back inside and fed him. We went to break-fast. I remember it as very tasty sausage and hot cakes with plenty of butter and hot maple syrup. We watched out the café windows for the sun to come out or for it to start snowing again. It did neither, and the cold grayness of the day cast its spell over us.

We faced a straight shot of about sixty miles from Dawson Creek to Fort St. John where my Alaska guidebook said there was a good road house. I didn't know exactly what a roadhouse was, but I figured we could find a warm bed and a meal there. But we needed to make more miles if we could, and I set my daily goal at Watson Lake, Yukon. The road, unpaved though it was, promised to be smoothly covered with ice and compacted snow.

Confidently, we loaded the Blazer, Chris beside me on the front seat and Bummer behind me on the lateral back seat, looking over my shoulder. We started toward Fort St. John from Mile One on the two-lane Alcan Highway. It was very cold and still. There was no traffic in either direction. The road had been freshly plowed with deep snow on either side of the highway. We were moving along in four-wheel drive. Immediately, we came upon the rear of an eighteen-wheeler doing a steady twenty-five miles per hour. I followed him for about an hour before I decided the road was straight and level and traction seemed positive. I decided to pass, though the road was narrow and the truck was laying out a cloud of snow.

I turned on my left turn signal, pulled to the left lane, and accelerated. The Blazer held steady on the hard packed snow. I pulled alongside the semi and pushed for more speed. We were close to the side of the trailer when the truck skewed slightly to the left.

I reacted automatically by jerking the wheel to the left. Our left front wheel dug into the snow at the edge of the road, and we were thrown off the edge and down onto the lower ground below the road. I think I said a prayer for soft snow. The Blazer buried itself over the hood in light powder.

I sat looking at the snow covering the windshield and said a short prayer.

"Oh, Lord. Let this not be the end of things."

I looked over at Chris. He was frightened but not hurt.

"You okay, son?"

"Yes, Daddy. I'm okay."

I looked back at The Bummer. He was legs akimbo against the back of my seat. He jumped up, whimpered, and licked my face. I felt him all over and found no broken bones.

Because I was less a man of introspection and more a man of action, I pushed against the driver's door. It gave way, against the light powdery snow, enough for me to get out. The quiet was near smothering. I made my way waist deep in snow to the highway. I looked back at the Blazer. I could barely distinguish between the white top of the truck and the surrounding snow. I nearly panicked. Chris and the dog were trapped inside a rapidly cooling vehicle.

My attention was drawn down the road where I discovered the eighteen-wheeler had stopped and begun to back. I watched thankfully as he approached me.

"I can pull you out." The driver opened his window and said. "But I won't be responsible for any damages to the vehicle."

I looked around. Our lives were in his hands. "Of course not. Just get me back on the road."

The driver dismounted and hooked a cable to my back bumper. He kept his engine running all the while. When he had remounted into the cab, he moved forward slowly, pulling the Blazer onto the highway. Then he was disengaged and off up the road before I had a chance to thank him.

In the silent, gray morning, we sat in the middle of the highway. I sat behind the wheel and tried to start the engine, but nothing happened. The cold was beginning to soak in. I had to move fast. First, I unrolled a U.S. Army Arctic down bag and helped Chris crawl into it in the back of the Blazer. Then I coaxed Bummer to join him in the bag. It seemed the dog understood the seriousness of the situation and readily crawled in with Chris.

Once I saw they were warm and comfortable, I thought about lighting a space heater and decided that was a bad idea. I'd save it until it was the last resort.

I opened the hood and beheld a snow-filled cavity. I would have to dig out the snow if I had any chance of starting the engine.

I donned Arctic mittens drawn at Fort Lewis and began digging the snow from around the fan. My hands soon lost their feeling. I realized I needed to start the space heater to keep my hands thawed out. I thought of a Jack London story where a man froze to death trying to light a fire in the forest.

I set out, hands numb now, to light the space heater in the back of the Blazer. After what seemed a very long time, I had a flame going in the heater.

"Hey, Chris, how you and the dog doing?"

"We're swell, Daddy."

My hands began to thaw. I went back to work, clearing snow from the engine, especially from around the fan. I figured rightly that if I could get the fan to spin, I might get the engine to start.

More than an hour went by. During this time, we had seen no one on the highway. Finally, after fifteen-minute shifts removing snow, followed by ten-minute shifts warming my hands, I thought the fan might be clear enough.

I checked to see that Chris and the dog were okay and then sat behind the wheel, crossed my fingers, and turned the key.

That gorgeous creature of a Chevrolet started right up. Chris and I cheered. Bummer howled. We let the engine warm a bit. When warm air began to flow through the cab, we set off again for St. John. The weather stayed overcast and cold—we're talking severe cold. I heard a noise like rocks bouncing up and hitting the underside of the fenders. Though we were on a solid surface of ice and snow, I kept hearing something bouncing off the fenders. I stopped to have a walk around to see if I could find anything wrong. I discovered that the plastic mud flaps I had bought in Puyallup had frozen and shattered leaving only jagged remnants of the original flaps.

I had been told not to pass a gas station, but I found that a lot of stations advertised in my guidebook were closed for the winter. I was glad I was carrying the two five-gallon jerry cans of gas on the roof. I hoped I wouldn't have to use them.

St. John wasn't much more than a café and a gas station. We, Chris and I, had a burger at the café. When we filled with gas, I let Bummer out to do his thing. He ran about, making his mark on every mound of snow. When I felt he had finished, I called him back. He immediately returned, jumped into the back of the Blazer, and settled down on the back seat. I gave him dog treat of rawhide to chew on, and he was happy.

Our goal for that day was the pass above Watson Lake, Yukon, where my guidebook said there was a roadhouse with restaurant and garage. Climbing toward the pass, we popped out of the clouds into a sun that seemed to warm us, though it remained very cold.

We reached the summit at near sundown and parked in front of the café. We were really hungry, and I felt that Bummer was hungry too. We went inside to an empty dining room. A woman came out of the kitchen to greet us, and seeing the dog sitting in the vehicle outside, she said, "Oh, it's too cold to leave that poor dog outside. Bring him in immediately."

"You sure?" I said.

"Yes, of course. Bring the dog inside."

Gratefully, I went outside and brought Bummer inside where Chris was seated at a table against the window. The dog immediately lay down beneath the table and appeared to go to sleep. We all enjoyed the warmth of the café.

The waitress came to the table holding menus, which she held sacrosanct and placed a cup of steaming coffee in front of me. "I'll bet," she said, "that young fella would like hot chocolate with whipped cream. Am I right?"

I looked at Chris. He nodded his head and smiled.

"Hot chocolate it is. Call me Ruthie. Now I see from your license plate you're Americans. Am I right?"

I nodded my head and smiled. I hoped she wouldn't hold it against us.

"May I ask what in the world are you three guys doing in the middle of the Yukon at this time of year?"

I looked at Chris.

"We're goin' to Alaska," he said.

I explained that I was a soldier and we were headed for duty in Anchorage.

"And the dog?"

"He's part of the family."

"I can get him some food if you want."

"He'll be fine. I have dog food in the truck. We're hoping to stay the night."

"Oh, sure. I'll let Doug know. He'll get a room warmed up for you."

"Doug?"

"He owns the place. Now I can let you search the menus, or I can offer you thick, juicy T-bone steaks. Being as your Americans, I expect you'll go for the steaks. Am I right?"

I looked at Chris.

He nodded with enthusiasm and licked his lips. "Yum."

"That's three votes for steak," I said. "I know the dog is already tasting the bones."

"Two steaks it is. I only know how to cook it rare or medium rare. Which'll it be, 'ey?"

"Medium rare for both of us, Ruthie."

"Two steaks, medium rare it is." Ruthie refilled my coffee cup before retiring to the kitchen.

Soon, the aroma of grilling beef filled the dining room. We salivated in anticipation.

An eighteen-wheeler approached from the north and pulled up in front of the café. The driver dismounted and hurried into the café. He stamped his feet. "Gonna be another cold one. Draw me a hot java, Ruthie," he called. He sat on a stool at the counter.

The waitress appeared, coffeepot in hand, poured a cup for the driver, and came over to refill my cup.

"Thanks, Ruthie." Using her name made me feel somehow like a member of the club.

The driver ordered hot apple pie "a la mode," took a long swig of hot coffee, and turned toward us.

"Say, I see from the license plates you're up from Washington. What's the road like south of here to Dawson Creek? It's smooth sailing north of here. The road crew's kept the highway clear all the way to Whitehorse."

While he munched his pie and drank his coffee, we shared small talk. He was headed for Edmonton. When our steaks were served, he said, "Wow, my mouth is watering. Those steaks sure smell good."

All the while, he never noticed Bummer sleeping under the table.

Chris and I dove into the T-bone steaks. They were like heaven. The driver finished his snack, dropped some money on the counter, and made to leave. "So long, Ruthie. See you next trip." He stepped over to our table. "That steak looks way too big for a little feller like you. I think I better take it off your hands." He smiled as he made to take the plate away from Chris. He was just making a joke, but The Bummer didn't do jokes well.

The driver stiffened, and his face paled. His smile disappeared. I looked under the table and saw Bummer had grasped his leg at boot top level and, while not biting down, was showing all his teeth and growling.

Chris wrote: *I always felt safe when Bummer was around. It was like having my own protection agency in one primeval yet totally loyal ball of furry fury. On one occasion during our trip north, we stopped for a meal at a roadhouse. Dad bought Bummer in with us, and he lay at our feet under the table concealed by the table cloth. We ordered steak. A trucker came into the restaurant and bellied up to the bar. I could feel more than hear a deep growl from under the table. I don't know why, but I was afraid of this man. When the steaks arrived, I saw before me a nice juicy T-bone. The trucker stood above me and declared I was too small for such a large steak. He reached for it. I heard Bummer growl, and quicker than I can tell it, the dog grabbed the trucker. The trucker ran out the door, jumped in his truck, and was gone down the road before I could think.*

"Drop, Bummer. Drop," I shouted and the dog let go of his grasp on the driver's leg.

Without further word, the driver hurried out and, mounting his cab, sped off down the road.

"Well, if that don't beat all," Ruthie said, laughing from behind the counter. "Never seen him move that fast. That's the funniest thing I seen all month. Desert's on the house."

9

We pulled the Chevy around to the side of the roadhouse, plugged the Blazer into a pole, and settled into a warm room at ground level. We gave the steak bones to Bummer, and he spent the evening chewing them up.

We went to sleep hearing the comforting sound of a 20K generator humming in the background. Sometime in the middle of the night, I woke when the generator shut down. I wasn't worried. I figured it just needed refueling. It would restart soon. I drifted off to sleep but again awakened to a rapping at the door. The generator was still shut down, so I knew there was trouble. It was cold. I opened the door to a man who introduced himself as Doug. "Sorry to bother you, but our generator conked out, and I brought a space heater to keep you warm until morning when I can get'er goin' again."

He placed the heater in the middle of the floor and lit the flame.

"What about my truck?" I said.

"No problem. I'll come by in the morning and thaw it out for you."

He left leaving me wondering about how he was going to thaw out the Chevy next morning.

The sun rose about ten o'clock on the first clear day we were to see in the Yukon. The space heater had kept us warm all night. The generator was still silent. I opened the front door to bone-chilling cold. I looked at the truck. She was covered in frost.

Chris and I cleaned up and dressed to go to breakfast. Someone knocked on the door. When I opened it, Doug said, "I'm here to thaw out your truck."

"We were just going to breakfast."

"Fine. You go ahead. By the time you're finished, I'll have her warmed up and ready to go. Can I have your truck key?"

Chris, Bummer, and I filed out of the room. Bummer didn't like the look of Doug. He growled as we walked around the front of the roadhouse to the door of the café.

"C'mon in," Ruthie said. "I got the kerosene stove going and ham and eggs in the skillet. Want coffee?"

"You bet. And hot chocolate for the boy."

When we had finished and said our goodbyes to Ruthie, we walked back around to the Blazer. Doug was still underneath the vehicle applying a blowtorch to the transmission. The engine was running, but she would not shift.

We packed our gear and waited to load the Blazer. I was afraid she'd catch fire any time.

"Go ahead and see if she'll shift gears now," Doug said.

I tried and she readily shifted through the gears.

"Looks like she's good to go. What do I owe you for the room?"

"Not a Canadian dime. I'm only sorry to have inconvenienced you. Please spread the word about my service as you go north."

We shook hands, and I started off north. The day was clear and cold. We dropped down out of the mountains and drove along Watson Lake. I stopped along the lake to let Bummer out to do his thing. He sniffed around a bit then hiked his leg up. Everything was still. There was no wind. The only sound was the dog prancing through the snow. Every once in a while, he would stop and listen. Then he'd jump up and nosedive into the snow. We guessed he was hunting for small animals.

"Look, Daddy," Chris said. He pointed out across the lake. "There's a bunch of dogs on the lake."

I looked and saw a pack of wolves crossing the ice.

"Those aren't dogs, son. They're wolves, and I think it's time for us to go."

We loaded up and continued up the Alcan Highway, deeper into the Yukon. Our destination for the day was Teslin. My guidebook said there was a fair-sized roadhouse there. The road was smooth-packed snow as it had been all the way so far. I never saw any road crews. I reckoned they must work all night long to keep the roads open during the day. It grew dark around 3:00 p.m. and began to snow. We arrived in Teslin around 5:00 p.m. and stopped in front of the roadhouse. We left the dog in the Blazer and entered the café to sit at the only unoccupied booth. The place was filled with native Indians, and we found it difficult to adjust to the noise of a room full of people talking and laughing after the last few days of quietness beyond the hum of our 350 hp Chevy engine.

A man walked up to our table and placed menus in front of us. He was a large man with graying hair and, from the sound of his voice, a Scandinavian.

"We're looking for a room for the night."

"Yaw, sure. We got rooms, you bet."

"We'd like to eat and then look at the rooms if you don't mind."

"Yaw, yaw. Eat and then we look. Coffee?"

"Yes, and some hot chocolate for the boy."

"Comin' right up." He went back behind the counter.

We studied the menus, and I decided on fried chicken. "See anything you like, son?"

"I don't know, Daddy. What are you gonna have?"

"I like the fried chicken."

"Oh, yum, yum. Me too, Daddy. Sure is noisy in here, isn't it?"

"Yeah, lots of people. We won't let them bother us, will we, son?"

He shook his head.

The chicken was beautifully prepared, and when we had finished, the waiter who introduced himself as Eric, the owner of the roadhouse, took us back to show us a room with two beds and a bath.

"Yes, this will do fine. I have a dog. Do you mind?"

"No, I don't mind. Just as long as he don't want no bed."

I laughed. "The floor is good enough for him. How much. American?"

"Let's see." He scratched his jaw. "American, hmm, that'll be twenty dollars."

I reached for my wallet.

He raised his hand. "Pay me at breakfast."

We brought the dog in and settled down for a noisy night. We hadn't been informed of a dance hall situated just outside our window. The music lasted until the wee hours. Around midnight, I got up and took the dog out one last time. It was still snowing, and after Bummer had lifted his leg several times on piles of snow, a native woman came out of the dance hall.

"Oh, nice doggie," she said. She was obviously drunk and staggering slightly. I snapped a leash on the dog. "Oh, nice doggie." She approached us and held out her hands.

"Lady, please leave the dog alone. He is not friendly."

Bummer strained on the leash. I tried to steer him around her and take him back inside.

"Nice doggy." She insisted on approaching, and stroking the dog who was growling now, his hackles raised.

"Okay, if you insist. Don't say I didn't warn you." I released the dog from his leash. He growled and sprang at the woman. The last I saw of her, she was jumping over a bank of snow, Bummer in hot pursuit. I waited a few minutes and called for the dog to come.

He hopped back over the bank and ran up to me panting, tongue lolling. I would have sworn he was grinning. The native woman was nowhere to be seen. I hurried the dog back into our room and hoped I would not receive a call for the rest of the night.

The next morning at breakfast, I paid for the room, and we beat a hasty retreat out of town. I was surprised. We'd had a good foot of powder snow drop on us last evening, yet the roads had been plowed to a smooth crust. We had yet to see a plow on the road. We had rarely seen any vehicle on the road. We learned later that we had made our trip during record cold and snowfall.

We worked our way to Whitehorse, Yukon Territory through what must have been farmland in summer. The road took a ninety-degree turn right and then left and right again every few miles. I took this to mean the road right of way zigzagged along boundaries through farmland, hidden by snow by the winter scape.

We kept the Blazer in four-wheel drive at thirty-five miles per hour under cloud cover for some miles. I saw a vehicle coming fast in the rearview mirror. It passed us doing maybe fifty, and I saw it was a new model sedan with three or four passengers. At the next nine-ty-degree turn, we found the car buried up to its windshield in snow.

"Hey, son," I said, slowing pulling up behind the car. "We know what that's about, don't we."

"Yes, Daddy. He's stuck."

"We can pull him out, can't we?"

Chris smiled and nodded.

I turned around so the back to the Blazer faced the car. I got out and hooked my tow chain to their back bumper. Then I pulled. The car came readily onto the road. The driver, a gray-haired man in a suit, thanked me as I derigged the chain. I noticed the other men in the car wore suits as well. That seemed strange this far away from anywhere. Chris, the dog, and I continued on our way up the high-way. Bummer grew restless, and I knew it was time for him to relieve himself, so I stopped alongside the highway and let him out to do his thing. He jumped from the back of the Blazer and hopped up onto the snow piled high at the edge of the road. He was soon hopping and diving into the snow, searching for voles. I called him back to the truck, and as he sprang back up into the back of the vehicle, I saw the car we had pulled out of the snow pass us by going too fast.

"I bet we see him again soon," I said to Chris.

"He's going too fast, isn't he, Daddy?"

I nodded as I remounted and started the Blazer. We continued north toward Whitehorse and soon came to a ninety-degree turn where we found the car again buried to its hood in the snow.

I stopped and walked over to the driver's door. The gray-headed man opened the car door and stepped out.

"Look, friend," I said. "There isn't much traffic on this road. You're the only other car I've seen. I'll pull you out once more, but if I come upon your vehicle stuck in the snow again, I'll pass you by. Fair enough?"

"Fair enough. Get me unstuck now, and you won't see me again, I promise."

I hooked him up and pulled him out onto the cleared road.

As I unhooked and stored the chain in the back of the Blazer, the man stepped out of the car and came back to shake my hand.

"I really appreciate it, my friend."

"No sweat. I hope you'll remember what I said."

"Indeed, I will." He returned to his car.

Chris and I continued on to Whitehorse and never saw that car again. I wondered what those men were about, but I had my own challenges to worry about.

10

We broke into sunshine that produced bare, black pavement on our approach to Whitehorse. We enjoyed a smooth ride into town under the sun. The temperature had warmed up to near freezing. We passed a Kentucky Fried Chicken restaurant on the near edge of town and continued on to scope out the city. Under its bed of winter snow, Whitehorse looked more like a blanket than a horse. There wasn't much going on in town, so I suggested we return to KFC and pig out.

"Oh, boy, Daddy. I'm all for that."

We returned to the sign with the goateed Kentucky gentleman and the white-and-orange bucket. I expected a taste of home as we entered the fast-food restaurant, and I wasn't disappointed.

"We'll have a bucket of chicken," I said to the young clerk.

He looked at me and then down at Chris.

"Ten pieces or more?"

I looked at the sign. "Eighteen pieces, please."

"Biscuits?"

"You bet."

"Mashed potatoes and gravy?"

"You bet."

"Coleslaw?"

I looked at Chris. He shook his head and grimaced.

"Naw, we don't need no stinking coleslaw."

The clerk laughed. "Hey, I just saw that movie *Treasure of the Sierra Madre* on TV. Wasn't Humphrey Bogart great in that?"

I thought for a moment. Then I remembered the Mexican bandit saying, "Badges? We don't need no stinking badges," and giving that wide gold-toothed grin. I looked at Chris. "'Member, Daddy? We saw that movie just a while ago."

"Oh yeah." We all laughed.

"That'll be $18.50."

"How much, American?"

The clerk punched buttons on his cash register. "$14.95. Do you need sauce?"

"I don't think so."

"Here or to go?"

"We'll eat here." I never gave the dog chicken bones, and I didn't want him sniffing around as we enjoyed our meal.

"Have a seat, and I'll bring your meal out to you."

We sat by the window, enjoying the sun. We were alone in the dining section. I wondered how the restaurant made it. I saw little traffic on the street. I guessed they got most of their business toward suppertime.

The chicken was fantastic. We ate most of it there. Mashed potatoes and gravy were always my favorite. Chris liked them too. Anything in gravy has always been my favorite.

I picked all the white meat off the last remaining breast, removed the skin and wrapped it in a napkin, and put it into a plastic bag. I planned to mix it with Bummer's chow that evening as a special treat. I placed the bag between the front bucket seats, and I could tell from The Bummer's interest, he could smell the chicken.

Soon after we left Whitehorse, we began to climb back into the mountains. The engine started to miss. We limped into Haines Junction at sundown where there happened to be a motel next door to a garage. We checked into the motel, and I asked about the garage.

"He's closed for the night, but I can call him if you need him."

"Please call him and tell him I need mechanical attention tonight if possible." I imagined a hefty bill for work after hours. "Tell him I can help if that works."

The motel clerk called the mechanic. "He says he'll come over after supper if you'll help."

We moved into a forgettable room and fed the dog before enjoying a forgettable meal at the local café. We arrived back at the motel just as the mechanic showed up. I backed the blazer into his garage. He fussed over the open hood and told me my fuel pump needed replacing. He'd have to order one from Whitehorse. They'd deliver it by air the next day.

We had a good sleep in a warm room. Bummer had bad dreams, howling and squealing the night long. We took him for a walk in the snow the next morning after a greasy breakfast. Bummer enjoyed himself stalking and diving nose first into the snow banks. I think he caught and ate two voles, though it might have been more.

That afternoon, the motel clerk phoned my room and told me the part had been delivered from Whitehorse and the mechanic would work on my Blazer after supper.

I joined him in the garage in the evening, and he began dismantling my failed fuel pump. I dug in the back of the Blazer and retrieved a fifth of Jack Daniels. I asked the mechanic if he'd like a drink. I can't remember his name, but we became close friends over that fuel pump and that bottle of whiskey.

My only memory of that night is that he charged me very little for the work and I went to bed drunk.

I woke early the next morning determined not to eat any more food in Haines Junction.

"Wake up, son. We gotta make tracks out a here. We'll eat breakfast on the road." We showered and dressed and started off down the road toward Kluane Lake, Yukon, and Alaska.

It had snowed again that night, and though the road had been plowed, we were surrounded by high banks of white powder. My guidebook showed a roadhouse with gas not far ahead. It reminded me to check my fuel level, and I was shocked to see we had less than a quarter of a tank. We pulled into the roadhouse through more than a foot of snow. Everything looked closed up. I made my way to the front door of the log house and knocked on the brass knocker. After three times, the door was answered by an elderly man in overalls.

"We're closed for the winter." He started to close the door.

"Wait. Please. Your advertisement in the book didn't say you'd close in the winter, and I don't have enough gas to make it to the next fueling station. Haven't you a few gallons you can sell me? I have my boy and my dog with me."

He looked out at the Chevy in the yard. "Boy? Dog? I'm just fixin' some breakfast, come on in and eat. Bring the dog in with you. My name's Ralph—Ralph McGuiness. Came here twenty years ago from Scotland." He offered his hand, and I was impressed by its roughness as we shook.

The three of us stepped into the roadhouse. There was a fire going in a large stone fireplace, and the room was lit by candlelight.

"Don't have much use for electricity in the winter. Try to save my fuel for emergencies. Usually, I stay open in the winter, but this year, we've had record snow and cold. Not much traffic, so I decided to shut her down." He seemed anxious to talk as he fried bacon and eggs on the gas stove.

We sat down in front of the fireplace at a heavy wooden table. Bummer lay under the table and went to sleep.

"Good-looking dog, he's got manners too. You up from the States?"

"Indeed, I am." The warmth of the room coupled with his warm attitude made me feel at home.

"Well-mannered boy too," he said, as Chris thanked him for his serving of the food.

Ralph sat and offered a blessing. The food was good.

"After we eat, I'll show you something in the barn. I think you and the boy will enjoy it. Have to leave the dog in here, though."

I was a little nervous about what he said and fingered my pistol in my vest pocket.

"Sure, but we can't stay long. Can you spare some gasoline?"

"I can spare you enough to get to Tok, on the Alaska side. They got year-round service there."

"Oh, great."

I didn't tell him the five-gallon cans I kept on the roof of the Chev for emergencies was full.

After breakfast, Ralph showed us out to the barn. I kept him in front of me, still not able to trust him.

"Here's my girl Bernice."

He led us into the barn where, nestled in straw, we found a beautiful Saint Bernard, suckling eight pups. Ralph dropped to one knee and hugged the dog close. The pups swarmed around him. Chris smiled and knelt beside Ralph to play with them.

"I thought you'd enjoy them. I surely do."

I took my hand out of my vest pocket. I realized that Ralph was just a good-hearted soul.

We went back into the kitchen for another cup of coffee.

"I'd be pleased if you could stay the night." Ralph was obviously lonely. "I'm a good cook, and there'll be no charge for the room."

I looked at Chris. He smiled and nodded. "Sounds like an offer we can't refuse."

Ralph and I went outside to fill the Blazer with gas from a hand-operated pump.

"That ought a do you until you reach Tok."

"How much?"

"No charge if you stay the night."

We stayed all day, helped him with his chores, and settled into a room for the night. Ralph watched with delight as Bummer hunted in the field behind the lodge and caught several voles.

"That'll do him for chow today," I said, as we returned to the barn to feed Bernice.

"Grab a few logs for the fire tonight."

We walked inside, Chris carrying more than his share: three logs. I carried four, and Ralph came behind with a sled bearing a dozen or so logs for the fire. That night, it was clear and cold. I marveled at the number of stars in the sky. I had never known there were so many.

"Yes," Ralph said. "Some people aren't satisfied with just seeing them but have to learn their names. I'm just satisfied with seeing them and knowing I share the universe with them."

We enjoyed a supper of venison and reconstituted vegetables. Ralph proudly offered a fresh baked apple pie. After supper, we sat around the fireplace. Ralph and I drank coffee. Chris slurped a hot chocolate.

"Mind if I smoke?" Ralph said, holding up a white-bowled pipe.

"Not at all."

"I like Glenn Miller. If you don't mind, I'll put on some records, and then I'll bring in the dogs. If you think the malamute will stand for it, I'd like to bring Bernice and her pups in to enjoy the fire for a while."

I hesitated.

"Well, please bring them in. If there's trouble, I'll put the dog in the truck."

Ralph donned his parka and mukluks and went outside. I leashed Bummer and held him close.

"Bummer, my good boy, good boy." I stroked his thick coat.

When Ralph returned with Bernice, followed by her pups, I felt Bummer tense up.

"No, Bummer. No, boy. Stay."

Bernice came right up to Bummer. He seemed startled by the size of her. She stood a good head taller than he. She nosed up to Bummer and chuffed. I felt him relax. I gave him slack. The two dogs circled and smelled each other's private parts. Bummer whined. I let him loose. The pups surrounded him. One, braver than the rest, approached Bummer and licked his nose. Surprised, Bummer backed and bared his teeth. I made to pull him back, but Ralph placed a hand on my arm.

"It's okay, they gotta learn."

I sat back, and soon, all the dogs were sprawled on the carpet before the fireplace. Bummer took a great deal of pleasure in the pups climbing over him, yipping and nipping him in play.

"I've never seen him like this," I said.

We all joined the dogs on the floor and played with them. Each time the fire crackled and threw sparks, the pups jumped up and ran around, yapping and crying. Bummer would stand and bark. The pups would gather below their mother's breast and feed a bit.

Finally, Chris yawned and fell asleep.

Followed by Bummer, I carried the boy up to bed.

"I've enjoyed this evening more than any this winter," Ralph said when I joined him for a nightcap by the fire. "Thank you so much for joining Bernice and me this night."

"It was my pleasure, Ralph. Now if you don't mind, I'll turn in."

The next morning, we said our goodbyes to our new Canadian friends with promises to maintain contact we knew we wouldn't keep and, with a full tank of gas, headed up the last few miles of Alcan Highway before we reached Alaska.

The sun shined brightly with a promise of spring that morning as we reached the Alaska border and pavement showing through the road melt. It was the first we'd seen, except for a few miles either side of Whitehorse since, it seemed, ages ago when we left British Columbia.

We pulled into Tok at midmorning and stopped at a real Chevron gas station with electric pumps and everything. An attendant rushed out to provide fuel. He was accompanied by two big Huskies, which, detecting our dog, circled menacingly around the Blazer.

Bummer was beside himself.

"Say, bud, fill her up," I said dismounting the Chevy. "Will your dogs fight?"

"Oh yeah. They fight all the time."

The attendant removed the cap and, plunging the pump into it, pumped fuel into our tank.

"I got a dog inside who needs to relieve himself."

"Yeah, so?"

"Could you put your dogs up long enough for him to do his business?"

"Tell you what, friend. Those dogs go wherever they want. I have no control over them."

I walked to the back of the truck. "Okay, friend, if that's the way you want it, but don't tell me I didn't warn you."

I opened the rear panel. Bummer launched himself out and made for the huskies. They circled briefly. Bummer made for their throats. They beat a hasty retreat around the back of the gas station, Bummer in hot pursuit.

"Well, I'll be doggoned," the attendant said. "I never seen them dogs run off like that before. That'll be $23.80. Want me to check your oil?"

"No, thanks." I handed him my credit card. Bummer appeared and, tongue hanging, jumped back into the back of the Chevy. He looked pleased with himself."

Chris wrote: *We stopped for gas. As was usual, everything was covered with snow. Dad asked the attendant if he could let Bummer out to go to the bathroom. There were at least two huskies, maybe three, circling the Blazer and smelling for our dog. The attendant said, "Sure, but my dogs aren't very friendly. You'll have to do this at your own risk." For the first and only time I can remember, I was afraid for Bummer. Those huskies looked mean. Dad let Bummer out. Bummer exited on the run and chased those dogs behind the gas station. After some sounds of conflict, there was only silence. Bummer emerged, relieved himself against the gas pump, and jumped up into the back of the Blazer. He was unscathed, and I swear he was smiling. I never doubted his ability again.*

I drove away, watching the gas station attendant remove his wool cap and scratch his head. I never saw anything else of his dogs.

It was here we left the Alcan Highway and headed south toward Anchorage on the Richardson Highway. Our goal for the day was Glennallen, where there was supposed to be a historic roadhouse. My guidebook told me these Alaskan roadhouses, some of them close to a hundred years old, had been placed some twenty miles apart, the distance a dog sled team could be expected to make in a day. Most had fallen into disrepair after World War II, but some like the Glennallen Roadhouse had survived, and were in business to this day.

We drove all day through the snow-covered mountains until toward sundown, in the habitually white scape, we arrived at a two-storied building of rough timber boards that appeared to have some years on them. There were several cars and pickups parked outside, and we heard music from inside as I told Chris to wait for me in the truck.

I stepped inside to a western movie set. Two sets of double doors kept the cold weather from a weathered hotel lobby. Ahead and to the left was a scarred hotel desk. Behind it sat a clerk in a sweat suit. Loud music emanated from a double doorway to the right. I looked in on an empty bar. A dated jukebox was playing an Elvis Presley tune—*Don't You Step on My Blue Suede Shoes*. A stairway behind the desk led to an upper floor. The lobby was filled with rustic furniture. Against one wall, a large stone fireplace, above which was mounted a gigantic moose head, glowed with burning embers. On a near wall was a large caribou head. At the rear of the lobby, a doorway led into the dark.

"What can I help you with, bud?"

"I need a room for the night—a quiet room for two and my dog."

"Sure." The clerk glanced at the door to the bar. "I got a quiet room on the second floor in a back corner. It's a little warm up there, but you can open a window if you want. A double is thirty bucks a night, ten dollars extra for the dog."

"Fine. You got a restaurant separate from the bar?"

The clerk pointed to the rear of the lobby. "Restaurant opens at sundown—about a half hour from now. Better make a reservation. This place will be full in an hour."

I looked at him. "You kidding me?"

"Wait. You'll see. We're in the middle of caribou season. You want reservations or not?"

"Sure. Make it six o'clock for two."

The clerk made a note. "Six it is."

I paid him.

"Here's the key to room 201 up the stairs and at the end on the right. Need more than one key?"

"No, thank you. You do serve breakfast, don't you?"

"Of course. Whaddya think this is, Canada?" He laughed and handed me the key.

I walked outside. "C'mon, son, we got a place for the night." I opened the back and grabbed our duffel. Bummer ran to a post and hiked his leg against it. I knew I'd have to take him out again later after he ate to do his final ablutions. We entered the roadhouse and climbed to the second floor and down the hall to room 201. We entered to find ourselves in a corner room with two double beds and a bath with shower. As advertised, the room was overheated. I opened a window on the setting sun. The inner window was covered by a storm window, which was sealed and covered with ice. The room cooled quickly.

We settled in, showered, and—near 6:00 p.m.—walked down to the dining room, leaving Bummer in the room. As advertised, the dining room was filled with people. A waitress showed us to a table close to the fireplace.

"My name's Alice. I figured you just came from outside, so you'd want to be warm. Was I right? Can I get you a drink?"

"You were right, Alice, and you can get me a bourbon and water. This is my son, Chris. He'll take milk. What's good for dinner?

"You bet. He'll eat the same as me."

"Then you'll want either the Kansas City cut or the porterhouse. The KC is our featured dinner. Comes with mushrooms and mashed potatoes and a salad. Drinks are included."

"I'd love the KC strip, but we have a dog upstairs expecting us to bring him bones, so I guess I'll have to settle for the porterhouse. What about you, son."

"Tell you what," Alice said. "I usually save all the bones for my sled dogs, but I'll keep three or four of them out for your dog if you want the strip steak and believe me you do."

"You got a deal, Alice."

She smiled and the boyish look gave way to a pretty, no a handsome face, vaguely reminiscent of Ingrid Bergman in *Joan of Arc*, but ridden hard and put away wet.

We took off next morning under fair skies and followed the Matanuska Glacier down out of the mountains toward Palmer, a few miles north of Anchorage. The wind was behind us all the way, and when we stopped for gasoline in Palmer, I was surprised to see I still had three quarters of a tank. Bummer headed for a snowdrift to relieve himself.

We finished our trip at the Fort Richardson front gate and checked into the VOQ (visiting officers quarters) on March 5, 1972. Ours was a two-room suite on the second floor of a wood frame building. It was called the igloo, so when I called Brenda to let her know we had arrived safely and told her we were ensconced in the igloo, she assumed the worst. We ate dinner in the officer's club— steak for both of us. We brought the bones to the igloo for Bummer. The night was cold, and we took Bummer out onto a snow-covered and crusted field. We stood in the snow and admired the high dome of stars above us. A streak of magenta light splashed with red and orange filled the northern quadrant.

"Ooh. What's that, Daddy? Fireworks?"

"That's the northern lights."

"What makes them?"

"I'm not sure. You'll have to study up on them and advise me."

"Okay."

Chris wrote: *We made it to Alaska having had an amazing adventure. We all bonded in a way I don't think many get to experience. Bummer was more than a pet. He had become a friend, protector, brother.*

"Let's get inside now. Tomorrow is going to be a busy day." I called the dog, and together, we headed inside. The building was of WWII vintage, but it was well maintained and G.I. spotless.

We unpacked and got ready for bed. Bummer curled up on a rug and very soon was chasing critters in his sleep.

"First thing tomorrow, we have to get you enrolled in school."

Chris wrote: *A lot of snow had fallen on Fort Richardson that year, and every day was an adventure in the woods behind our house. Dad enrolled me in school, and he met me every day after school until my mom and sisters arrived. One day before, I had said it would be fun to have Bummer pull me on skis. Next day, when I got home, Dad met me at the door with two pairs of cross country skis. "Let's take these skis out for a test drive." He showed me how to put the skis on, donned his skis, grabbed Bummer's leash, and led us to the backyard. Dad handed me the leash and said, "Hang on." He started off. Bummer followed, pulling me. I think Bummer realized what was happening because he started off fast. What fun. I stumbled several times and finally fell in the snow. I think Bummer had tired and threw me intentionally. This was not the last time we did this. I think Bummer enjoyed it more than I did. I showed my sister Evelyn how to do it, and we let Bummer pull us through the snow many times during the following years. Looking back, I think Bummer could have been a world-class sled dog.*

"Aw, gee, Daddy. I guess our adventure is over."

"On the contrary. Our adventure is just beginning. You and I, your mother and sisters have so much to learn about The Great

Land. After we get you in school, we have to go to housing and apply for our new home. Here is the elementary school." I pointed to a spot on the map of the post. "And here is the housing office." I identified the several other buildings I needed to visit to complete my in-processing. I'd need to register Bummer with the post veterinarian. I'd need to register my vehicle and obtain post tags as well.

The vet told me the post rules governing pets were stringent. I should maintain strict control over the dog at all times.

Chris wrote: *We lived in a two-story eight plex. Across the street from our backyard was a patch of woods where I spent a lot of time. Bummer broke his chain a lot and spent time there too. He had a brilliant white tip on the end of his tail. It seemed to offer a banner for all to see. Whenever a military police cruiser approached, he dropped his tail behind a bush. When the cruiser passed, up came his tail. He only did this when the MPs were around.*

Lots of kids and animals would cut corners around our house. Bummer ambushed lots of cats that way. My friend Jimmy ran around the corner of our house and surprised Bummer so that he was bitten on the leg. Jimmy's parents reported the incident to the MPs. This was Bummer's second offence, so by POST Regulations, he was to be put down. An MP was dispatched to pick up the dog and deliver him to the vet for execution. Evelyn and I were distraught at the thought of losing Bummer. We wailed and pulled fur from his coat and began filling a shoebox so we'd have something to remember him by. The MP showed up and was so taken by Evelyn's lamenting, she stated she could not do this and granted Bummer a stay of execution.

11

Bummer was a mature adult by the spring of 1972. Our family was assigned quarters in an eight-plex courtyard containing four-bedroom town houses where there were lots of kids. We were not allowed to fence the yard. The dog needed to be chained up whenever he was outside. He seemed to accept this rather philosophically, for a dog, and perhaps saw himself as the guardian of the family. At the same time, he never acted like a dog and appeared driven by the wolf blood in him.

He never made friends with any dogs that we knew of, though once, with Evelyn's instigation, he got loose and mated with a neighbor's dog. The bitch had a fine litter of little Bummers. He had more than fifty fights with other dogs that I knew of during his long lifetime, never lost one and never bore scars from his adventures.

While he never killed another canine, cats were quite another story. Soon after we moved onto Fort Richardson, the cat population began to decrease despite the fact we kept the dog chained whenever he was outside alone. When a neighbor would complain that our dog had killed their cat, our answer was always, "The leash laws apply to all pets."

I wondered how The Bummer was able to amass this casualty rate until one day, I observed a cat walk tauntingly just beyond the length of the dog's chain where he lay on the grass apparently asleep. What the cat didn't notice, but I witnessed, was the dog inching slowly backward to create slack in the chain. When the cat approached to a point just opposite the dog's head, he sprang forward and broke the cat's back with one quick snap of his jaws. All this happened so fast, I wasn't sure I'd seen it. I went outside. Bummer sat up and looked at me innocently. Just beyond him was a dead cat.

"Well, you certainly are a bummer, aren't you, boy?" I knelt and scratched him behind his ears.

I worried about how the dog would react to encounters with large animals, a common occurrence in Alaska. This proved unnecessary because Bummer invariably gave bears and moose a wide berth. Whenever we came upon them in the woods, the dog would very quietly walk close on my heels.

Smaller wild animals were something quite different. When hiking in the woods with the dog, I was continually on the watch for porcupines and skunks. One time, while hiking to a favorite fishing spot, Bummer ranged ahead as was his style. Occasionally, he'd smell a ground squirrel of a vole and, digging him out, would gobble him up. This was the dog's only food when we were camping. When I saw him bolt off the trail toward the woods, I looked ahead and saw a huge porcupine heading our way. He was nearly as big as Bummer.

"Bummer. No. Bummer, come back here."

The dog ignored me but continued to gallop toward the porky. I watched fearfully. The porky stopped when he could see Bummer approaching. Porcupines are notoriously nearsighted. This one bristled, his long, sharp quills pointing forward. (They say porkies can actually launch their quills, but I believe these self-defense weapons simply come loose on contact with an enemy.)

Bummer suddenly applied the brakes, stopped short, and sauntered nonchalantly back to my side.

No fool, he.

We went camping whenever we got the chance. After a rainy Memorial Day and a leaky store-bought tent, Brenda refused to sleep on the ground anymore. I learned that the Air Force Special Services had tent trailers for rent, so I convinced her we should try that. We drove down to the Kenai Peninsula and camped by a lake. I discovered when I set up the camper that the tent canvas was torn away from the trailer nearly all the way around. That was okay until a storm with high winds and pelting rain came up during the night and—you guessed it—we all got wet.

Once more, Brenda put her foot down. "You can take the kids and the dog camping from now on. I'm not going to sleep wet and cold again."

I looked around for a camper trailer, small enough to go most anywhere, large enough to accommodate the five of us and The Bummer. I needed one that could serve simple needs and would be comfortable when we couldn't plug it in for electric power. After a lengthy search, I found what I believed would serve us perfectly: a sixteen-foot low liner in great shape. I showed it to Brenda, and she agreed to try it.

It worked perfectly, though the two little kids were a bit cramped in the upper bunk at one end of the trailer. Cindy slept in the lower berth. Brenda and I slept at the other end in a fold-down berth. The dog slept on the floor in front of the door.

Chris was the most uncomfortable, electing to sleep in a pup tent outside the camper, on our next trip. He changed his mind that night when it rained causing a river to run through his tent.

We liked to camp at established campgrounds with running water and electric hookups, but often, these were too crowded, so we'd elect to rough camp along a river or just in the woods where we could let the dog run free.

One of our favorite places to camp was a state campground called Nancy Lakes. While it was just a few miles north of Anchorage, we often had it to ourselves. The campground was on the banks of the largest of three lakes. I bought a canoe and often paddled some or all the family around the lake. Chris and I would carry the canoe over to the next lake, which held large rainbow trout. Bummer loved to ride in the canoe. He had a great sense of balance and could hop aboard and settle into the bow or into the center of it without rocking it at all. On landing, he'd invariably wait quietly while I dismounted and held the canoe steady for him to stand and jump out.

Chris wrote: *Dad would take us camping, fishing, cross-country skiing, and other activities all the time, and Bummer was always with us. I'd seen him jump from a canoe without getting me wet, and he'd even climbed back in a couple of times with my dad's and my help. I remember on one camping trip, we, my sisters and I, were having a moose turd fight with my dad. We were on a large rocky mound. I looked down into the valley below to see Bummer stalk, kill, and eat a rabbit. What a sight. It was remarkable what he could do. When in the woods, Bummer would revert to the wild and live off the land each day only to return to camp each night. We always packed his dog food only to have it eaten by the Canada jays we called "camp robbers." Bummer was self-sufficient.*

One time, while out camping, Dad and I went fishing. For whatever reason, Bummer was left in camp. When we returned, the dog made it quite clear he was not happy with me. He wouldn't allow me to pet him. Any look I gave him was met with a growl. I think he considered himself a member of our pack and higher in the pecking order than me. He soon forgave me, and we were brothers again.

The silver (coho) salmon runs, normally beginning in early September, were a time of frantic rushing up and down the one two-land highway between Anchorage and the Kenai River. It was the same during the king (Chinook) salmon run in May and the red (sockeye) salmon run in June. Rather than fight the traffic every weekend only to end up camping in a quarry with no ready access to fishing, we rented a camping spot on the Kenai River with access to all the runs during the too short summers.

I ran up and down the river seeking favored fishing spots in a fourteen-foot aluminum fishing boat with a fifteen-horse outboard. Bummer loved to ride in that boat. He'd lay on the center seat to avoid get wet or having a salmon landed on his carcass and go to sleep.

One year during the king run, I wanted to give Chris a chance to catch his first king salmon, so we anchored in the most favored spot on the river and planned to sit out all night to catch the early morning bite. I placed a float on the anchor rope, so if we hooked into a king, I could drop off the anchor to fight the fish and not lose my spot.

Darkness fell. The three fishermen who had shared the hole we anchored in had left for the night. It grew cold. Muscles cramped. We couldn't move around much. The only sound was the river running toward the sea.

"We better take a stretch break on shore and let Bummer do his thing."

It was around three o'clock in the morning. We'd not had a strike the whole night. I unhooked the bobber from the boat and started the outboard for the short sprint to shore. Stiff legged, we stood and stepped on land. Bummer hopped out, sniffed around, and hiked his leg against a bush. Then we returned to our vigil.

It grew light. We could see our breaths. I felt a tap—tap at the tip of my rod—and detected the soft pickup of my bait by a king salmon. I lifted the rod tip slightly and felt the fish start to move. I snapped the rod to set the hook. The fish ran downriver. The reel buzzed as yards of line began to pay out.

"Fish on!" I cried. This was the signal for Chris to reel his line in so as to avoid entanglement.

"Unhook the anchor, quickly, boy." Chris, sitting in the bow, dropped his rod in the boat and unhooked us from the anchor while I started the engine and followed the fish downriver. Drawing closer to the king while maintaining pressure on the line, it took to the air.

"Wow, Dad. That's a big fish."

I maneuvered the boat to coax the fish out of the current and into an eddy.

"You bet. It'll go sixty pounds at least. Hang on, he's making another run for it." Fifteen minutes later, the king was tiring and ready for the net.

"Kneel on the seat, son, and be ready to dip the net on the port side. As soon as the fish is in there, pass it to me. He's too big for you to handle."

"Bummer, down." The dog had stood up on the seat to see what was going on. He might jump overboard and try to help me land the fish. It was not a good idea in this swift river.

Chris guided the net over the king's head, careful not to hit it with the rim. I stood in the back of the boat and took the handle of the net from Chris to lever the fish into the boat where I coldcocked him with my bat. Bummer sat up and howled. From somewhere close by, there was an answering howl, probably from somebody's husky, but possibly by a wolf.

"We better hurry back to our spot. This bite won't last long."

I powered the boat back to pick up the float. "Fish on!" Chris hollered not five minutes later and stood up to fight another king. I reeled in quickly and started the engine.

"Let go the mooring as soon as you can. Careful. Don't fall overboard."

This big fish made its initial run up river, and I followed it until it stopped to sulk on the bottom.

"Put some pressure on him," I coached the boy. "Don't let him rest up."

Chris began pumping his rod as he reeled in.

The king began to run downriver. I worked to coax it into the slower running shallows. Thirty minutes later, we had the fish in the boat. It was getting crowded. I hurried back to our mooring. Two fishermen had pulled into the hole as the sun came up. I hooked back up to our bobber, and we dropped our baits back into the water.

"Well, you got your first king salmon. Congratulations, son." I shook his hand as he admired the big fish.

When I was certain the morning's bite was over, I headed for our campground and a hot coffee. When we weighed our fish, mine was sixty-five pounds. Chris's was just over forty.

During my eight years of service in Alaska, Chris, Bummer, and I shared many fishing adventures like this one.

12

Captain Gil Randall was a light-skinned Cajun. He was, I think, more than six feet tall, strong as an ox. He must have weighed in excess of 250 pounds. There was not a visible ounce of fat on his body. He could have crushed me with one blow, but I think it never occurred to him.

He had black eyes, coal black hair, and a deep, not necessarily southern sounding, voice. He came to the Alaskan Brigade shortly after I did and was assigned the adjutant's position. The unit adjutant or administrative officer issues orders in the name of the commander. He is universally disliked. Gil had a personality to match his job.

Gil was one of those combat veterans suffering from PTS who never made it all the way back. His wife had left him while he was in Vietnam. I was the only friend he had.

For some reason, we hit it off. I can't remember how it came about, but I agreed, one weekend, to go fishing with Gil.

That first year, we hit mostly dry holes. We didn't understand that the trout and the salmon ran during specific times, and the waters were otherwise devoid of fish with some exceptions. Grayling and Dolly Varden trout were available almost any time of the year.

Gil and I enjoyed fishing together, even though that first year, we were mostly zeroed out. Bummer accompanied me most of the time. I won't say he liked Gil but he tolerated him. And Gil just tolerated Bummer.

One day in May 1973, when the spring king salmon run was on, Gil came down to my office.

"The king salmon run is starting in Deep Creek and the Ninilchik, just north of Homer. You interested in going down there with me?"

We'd have to leave right after work on Friday and drive down to Homer, some two hundred miles to get there in time for opening season at midnight, fish for a day and a half before driving the two hundred miles back to Anchorage and Fort Richardson. If we were able to catch one king weighing fifty pounds or more, it would be worth it.

"Lemme check with Brenda. I'm sure we got nothing going on this weekend. I'll take the Blazer. We can rack out in the back whenever we get too tired to fish."

"Right," Gil said shortly as was his way.

We hit the road after Friday's duty hours at about 1900 (7:00 p.m. to you civilians) and headed south for the Kenai Peninsula, Gil riding shotgun, me driving, and Bummer perched in the back seat. We arrived at Deep Creek around midnight, backed up to a sandbar, and started a fire to make some coffee. I had a feeling we were going to need it. Bummer dismounted and sniffed at all the bushes.

The creek was very shallow and fordable on foot at most places above its mouth in Cook Inlet. We started fishing in the darkest part of the night at that time of year—enough light to navigate the creek without falling. We waded up, and down the creek, Bummer fished with us. He was more in the water than out. He'd get soaking wet and roll in the sand so as to keep the mosquitoes away. The mosquito season had barely begun, so they weren't too thick. Later in June, we couldn't fish without wearing gloves and head nets. Bummer would often submerge himself in the water, just his eyes and nose above the surface, like a crocodile, to escape the bloodsucking insects that would sometimes drive moose and caribou mad. The only place I ever saw that was worse for mosquitoes was Northern Minnesota.

Around 0300, I began to peter out. I needed sleep.

"Hey, Gil. Pardner, I'm gonna rack out for a couple of hours. I've about had it."

"Okay, Dick. I'm gonna fish maybe another hour. Then I'll get some sleep too."

I dropped the tailgate on the Chevy and unrolled and unrolled my sleeping bag in the bed of the vehicle. I unrolled Gil's bag as well so he wouldn't have to wake me when he came to sleep. There was also the question of dominant terrain. I wanted to mark Gil's terrain so Bummer wouldn't occupy it and cause a ruckus whenever Gill showed up.

These things accomplished, I crawled into my bag and invited Bummer to board. He did so, smelling of wet dog, and sprawled out beside my bag.

I slept.

I was awakened by Bummer's low, dangerous growl.

"Arrr, what's goin' on," I managed to mumble.

"Your dog's in my sleeping bag. He won't get out."

I saw Bummer, curled up in Gil's sleeping bag—head lifted, teeth bared, and growling at Gil, standing at the tailgate.

I started to laugh but thought better of it even in the fogginess of exhausted sleep that 250 pounds of ragin' Cajun is not to be laughed at when he'd gone without sleep for more than twenty-four hours. On top of that, he'd caught no fish.

"Here, Bummer. Here, boy. Come on over and sleep with me." As the dog crept in beside me, the last thing I remember before I went back to sleep was that the dog had shed most of his sand, but he surely did stink.

Oh yes, one more thing. I remember hearing Gil mumble as he crawled into his bag, "This feels awful," before he began snoring.

This was the first of many fishing trips the three of us went on. Gil and the dog never accepted one another as friends, but they shared mutual respect. Gil Randall so loved The Great Land that, rather than leave, he surrendered his army commission to become a fishing guide on the Kenai River.

13

In the spring of 1975, I received orders for the U.S. Army Command and General Staff College at Fort Leavenworth, Kansas. This was advertised as the "best year of your career." It might have been, but I was too busy working on my master's thesis to notice. Our family would fly down to Kansas City, Missouri, together. Brenda and I discussed our options for Bummer—there was only one. We'd crate him up and fly him along with us. We were uncertain how well he would take to being confined in a crate for more than five hours, but he appeared to be just fine when we landed. Though, for some reason, the baggage handlers were overanxious to hand him over to me.

We signed into quarters at Leavenworth during the month of August. It was hot—hotter than any of us had known for some years. Our saving blessing was the central air-conditioning in our relatively new brick, two-story, four-bedroom duplex.

During the next couple of months, Bummer spent the majority of his time sleeping on the cooling register in the front hall. Whenever we took him for a walk, always on a leash as required by Army rules, his tongue hung nearly to the ground. He shed his outer coat rapidly.

With autumn came cooler weather and relief for all of us. I developed a daily routine of running several miles including an uphill run to an abandoned missile site. I took The Bummer along on these runs. Whenever we started up the hill to the missile site, I'd let Bummer run free in deserted woods. He ranged back and forth ahead of me into the woods on either side of the road, nose to the ground. He was happiest whenever it snowed.

When spring came with warming weather in 1976, I worried a little because one kind of creature, unknown to Bummer, dwelt in the woods. I feared he might encounter a rattlesnake or a copperhead, both of which inhabited the woods around here. My fears were soon realized.

One warm day in May, we were running up the hill that led to the missile silos. Bummer ranged through the woods as was his habit. He sounded off with a loud yelp and came running to my side.

"What's the matter, boy?" I stopped and knelt to check him out. I looked and felt over his coat from nose to tail but found nothing save a slight swelling on his face behind his jaw. Bummer was acting strangely subdued.

We continued up the hill, Bummer sticking close to my side. Very soon, he began to lag behind. His breathing became labored. I was sure he'd been bitten by a poisonous viper.

I slowed to a walk and turned toward home. With but a quarter mile to go, he lay down in the road and could not go on. I stooped and wrapped his limp body in my arms. I lifted all eighty-five pounds and carried him the rest of the way home.

"Brenda," I called for her as I turned up the walk to our house. "Brenda, honey, open the door," I called louder.

She opened the front door. "Oh, Dick, what has happened?"

I carried Bummer into the front hall and laid him on the register. "Snake bit, I think. We gotta call the vet."

I called the post veterinarian. "I have a dog who's been bitten by a snake, I think."

"What's he doing now?"

"He's unconscious, lying on the air-conditioning register. He seems to be barely breathing."

"Better get him here ASAP."

I hung up. "Honey, start the car." I had just bought a new Buick sedan. Brenda rushed ahead of me as I picked up the dog again and placed him on the back seat of the car.

"You know where the vet is?" I said.

"No. You'd better drive."

I got behind the wheel and sped up to the vet's office.

After the vet examined him and detected the place of the bite, he said, "Well, he surely has been bitten probably by a copperhead. Their venom is particularly strong this time of year. I'll give him a shot of antivenom. Keep him in a cool place with lots of water handy. In two or three days, we'll know if he's going to make it."

"What are his chances, Doc?"

"I give him fifty-fifty."

We laid him on the register and turned the air conditioner on high. He stayed motionless there for three days. We could hardly tell whether he was breathing or not. His heart beat weakly.

On the night of the third day, I was awakened by the sound I had been waiting to hear. It was the sound of a dog drinking water.

"What's the matter, Dick?" Brenda sat up in bed.

"It's Bummer. I think I hear him drinking water." I hastened down the stairs and into the front hall.

The dog had managed to turn onto his stomach and lift his muzzle to where he could dip his tongue into the water and scoop it up. He looked up and licked my hand. I knew he was going to make it.

"There, boy. That's a good boy," I crooned to him and stroked his fur. Tears of joy came into my eyes. Brenda joined me, followed by the children. We all knelt and thanked God.

A week later and we were running together again. The Bummer, thinner now, was his old aggressive self. When a beautiful Irish setter came to our front door, Bummer pounced on her and would have mauled her if she had not dropped to the ground and pleaded, belly up, not to be hurt. Bummer, who had not been neutered, sniffed her all over and let her go her way. Though he was sometimes seen as a mean dog, he was ever the gentleman toward beautiful female dogs.

One day, as we ran up the hill together, toward the missile silos, I spotted a garter snake dead on the road. I stopped and, stooping, pointed to the snake.

"Here, Bummer. Take a look at this."

The dog stopped at my side and stuck his nose down toward the snake. When he got the scent, he jumped three or four feet in the air, yelped, and hit the ground running toward home. Apparently, he'd learned his lesson about snakes.

14

As graduation day approached in June 1976, I was told to expect orders either to Department of the Army in Washington, DC, or to the Training and Doctrine Command at Fort Monroe, Virginia. I saw neither posting as pleasant or affordable to my family and me. On top of that, I was first and foremost a field soldier and found the idea of three years behind a desk on some general officer's staff distasteful. While I knew I had to do my desk time in order to progress farther along in the ranks, somewhere between Vietnam and the states, my priorities had shifted from career to family. Now I just wanted the best for my wife and kids—the dog too.

When the orders arrived, I couldn't believe my luck. While I was ordered to TRADOC (Training and Doctrine Command) headquartered at Fort Monroe, I was to posted to the Combat Development Activity in Fort Richardson, Alaska, to work on developing ways and means of conducting warfare in winter. This would dead-end my career progression in the Army, but it meant all to me and my family.

I looked forward to another trip up the Alcan Highway, this time during summer with wife, kids, and dog.

I went to see the Chevrolet dealer in Leavenworth. He was very kind and helpful to us when I explained my situation. He was willing to take my new Buick in trade for what I paid for it brand new.

"I'm looking for a four-by-four suburban and an eighteen-foot camper trailer."

"Do you really need four-wheel drive?"

"Well, now that I think about it, most places in Alaska, I can't go off-road. I think I only used four-wheel drive once with my Blazer, and that was in the PX parking lot."

"I can have a suburban built for you in Detroit with a nonslip transmission that'll take you anywhere you want to go and save you a thousand dollars. Now about the trailer. You'll appreciate having two axels over one because of the added stability. The shortest twin axel models come in twenty-foot lengths. Again, I can have a fine model constructed at the volunteer factory in Tennessee and delivered in time for you to leave for Alaska. While you may be the main driver of the suburban, I think your wife will want to be in charge of putting together the trailer. I think we ought to get her down here to finalize plans for its construction, don't you?"

The result was a perfectly matched pair of vehicles for the road and a beautifully designed home away from home, both delivered just in time to test drive before taking off for Alaska.

Our good friends, the McClures, had orders to Fort Richardson too, and we decided to convoy together. Phil had a wife and two kids and a dog. Our families got along well, but his dog, a springer spaniel, was crazy. Dandy was the only dog I can ever remember being afraid of. I never dared approach him. He had that insane look in his eyes and never showed the innate loving trust in humans most dogs have. We would have to work hard to keep the two dogs separated. Phil loved his crazy dog, though his family feared and despised him. I knew if they fought, The Bummer would certainly kill him. Phil would take it hard.

Our dog was six years old now and still just off the edge of wildness. We had been lucky with him so far, and while he continued to be aggressive with other dogs and willing to do battle in a heartbeat, he usually avoided contact with strangers and only tolerated those humans with whom we associated.

While he continued his distrust of other people, the dog loved the children, and they loved him in return. They had grown together from babies to adolescents. I think Bummer considered himself the shepherd of our entire family. He was always very protective toward Brenda and the children. He loved me but treated me as the alpha male. We always had to watch him very closely when other children came over to play. We feared a wrong move by another child might be misinterpreted as aggressive and that he would react to it. The few times he was thus challenged, he showed restraint—a warning growl and a look, or bared fangs was usually all it took to send the neighbor's children scurrying home. While he lived fourteen years, he seldom bit a human, though there are rumors he nipped or snapped at our kids occasionally, except once when he was very old, he bit me, but I think it was a mistake.

Soon after occupying new quarters at Fort Richardson, we learned that Keith Reid, my old fishing buddy from Fort Lewis, and his family had been assigned to the post. They lived just down the street from us. His wife Nellie and Brenda were best of friends. We agreed to get together over dinner very soon.

One warm afternoon, the front door open except for the screen, Keith showed up and, without preamble, walked into our house. Bummer launched himself at Keith who barely managed to escape being bitten or worse. The Bummer apparently remembered Keith from Fort Lewis and still didn't like him.

I said earlier that Bummer was respectful of the larger animals—bear, moose, and the like—and never created a scene when we encountered those creatures in the woods. He was smarter than most dogs and would act as if he didn't see a wild animal larger than himself, except one time when he saved me from being killed by a big brown bear.

One summer day, I had taken him to the far reaches of the northern end of Fort Richardson, close to Eagle River, in search of a good area to set up a compass course. It was rumored that a large grizzly bear (called simply "brown bear" in Alaska) frequented this area, but I didn't know about it then.

Bummer ranged out ahead of me as was his usual manner, searching for voles and such. After a while, he dropped back and followed close on my heels. I took little notice of it until a brown bear stood up on its hind legs directly ahead of us. It must have stood eight feet tall. I was aware that I was unarmed. Before I could react, the dog had taken up a position between the bear and me and was snarling at the bear.

"Bummer, no," I whispered as he moved forward, neck and back hairs bristling, teeth bared, snarling savagely.

The bear hesitated before dropping on four feet and disappearing into the woods.

I gathered the dog in my arms and hugged him tightly. "Bummer, you great dog you. You saved me that time. I owe you my life." Bummer acted as if nothing had happened, but I noticed he stayed close to me as we headed home.

He ignored other dogs unless they invaded his turf, and then he would attack immediately and decisively. Smaller wild animals like rabbits, voles, squirrels, and the like, he ate. I always worried about what he would do if confronted by a porcupine or a skunk. He had learned about porkies the easy way, and I can't remember his ever running afoul of a skunk.

The one thing he feared greatly, other than snakes, was the discharge of firearms. Once, while on a fishing trip with the dog and my dad, who was visiting from the lower 48, we chanced upon a fool hen. These birds, a kind of grouse, were called fool hens because they appeared to have no fear of humans. I had my .44 hog leg with me and decided the grouse would make a good meal, so I drew my pistol and shot the bird. It was the first time I ever discharged a firearm in the company of the dog.

Bummer bolted and raced back down the trail we had been following. Dad and I continued up the trail toward a river I planned to fish. When, a few hours later, Bummer hadn't shown up, I decided to head back to the Chev and begin a search for the dog. When we arrived at the suburban, we found Bummer hiding under the vehicle. I never fired a weapon around the dog again.

We had to keep him on a chain whenever he was outside our house alone. I knew he didn't like it, but he didn't object or howl. He accepted the restraint with dignity. He'd lie on the grass and watch the people and cars pass. Whenever a military police car went by, he'd retreat to a shady place between the back porch and the garage. How he knew the threat offered by the MPs, I'll never know.

Cats, on the other hand, were free to run loose. It never seemed fair to me—doesn't to this day, but there it is. It was the law. Cats didn't make noise, usually, unless they were in heat. Then we'd hear their howling all over the neighborhood. They urinated, defecated, and killed birds around the neighborhood without restraint. That they never ate their kill was sinful to me. But it is their nature.

Bummer loved to fish. He would openly stalk them in creeks and shallow water and dive after them. Sometimes, he was successful, though he never learned the rule of refraction; the fish was always farther away than it looked. He jumped among spawned out salmon and ate his fill.

We always treated Bummer like he was a house dog rather than an outside dog. He learned quickly to mind his indoor manners from the time I brought him into my home. He never bared his teeth at me, except once when he was very old, or mine. He never jumped up on any of the family and never jumped up on the table for food but crawled under the table and waited for one of us to drop something on the floor. This was perfectly acceptable behavior in my house.

On one single occasion, although it was never proved, Bummer violated house rules. I returned from fishing with a good catch of silver salmon and was preparing to smoke one of them. I split it down the middle, brined it for some hours, and laid the two halves on the kitchen table to air-dry. I was alone with Bummer on the bottom floor of the house. He lay sleeping in the next room. I stepped out onto the back porch to see if the smoker was ready. I was outside for maybe ten seconds.

I walked back into the kitchen to find one of the salmon halves missing. It had vanished in ten seconds time. I stared dumfounded at the remaining half salmon on the kitchen table. I turned to look at Bummer, who remained sleeping on the living room floor. He seemed not to have moved since last I looked his way.

I inspected the crime scene closely, looking for a clue, a scrap of salmon flesh or blood. I even smelled the dog's breath. It was as if one-half of my salmon had never existed. The only clue I had was the absolutely innocent expression on the dog's face. He had to have been the culprit, yet this was a mystery that has never been solved. Though he had many opportunities to repeat his crime, he never did.

Bummer remained a bachelor, except for that one occasion I mentioned earlier. I never wanted to have him neutered because I felt that would have diminished his presence as a half-wild animal.

Our family respected him as he was and didn't want him to change. We loved him, and he loved us. His wolfish nature blended perfectly with my sense of my own manhood. I was a soldier, a ranger, and a paratrooper. My manhood was in synch with The Bummer as it was in synch with my family.

15

If Bummer loved anything more than the summers in Alaska, it was the winters. He loved to run and jump in the snow hunting for the small creatures that made up his picnic menu. The kids called it "making tunnels in the snow." What The Bummer liked more than anything was the whole family having a frolic in the snow. We'd have snowball fights on skinny skis and then doffing the skis roll with him in the snow. He loved it.

I've always thought I had a special affinity for dogs. I often hear people say, "Well, I'll be. He (or she) has never taken to a stranger like he has to you." Though dogs seem to sense my feelings for them, they have not always responded in a positive way.

The strangest and scariest encounter I ever had with dog occurred during my second tour in Alaska during one gray day that promised snow. It occurred near my home on the military reservation at Fort Richardson, in the foothills of the Chugach Mountain Range, near Anchorage.

It was Thanksgiving Day. My wife had a turkey roasting in the oven. I decided rather than sit around smelling the feast being prepared, stomach grumbling, I'd go for a short ski.

The previous night's weather offered an inch of powder on a solid base of a yard of more of compact snow. The morning offered ideal conditions for cross-country skiing.

"Anyone want to go skiing? Cindy? Evelyn? Chris? Bummer, you surely want to go out in the snow with me, don't you?"

They all preferred to sit around smelling the turkey cooking. Bummer, usually eager to hit the trail, was also reticent this day. He seemed to enjoy the aroma of smelling turkey like a Turk likes the smell of tobacco.

I stepped out on the back porch alone. The temperature was hovering around twenty degrees Fahrenheit, perfect for a morning's ski. Once more, I tried to coax Bummer out into the snow, and once more, he ignored me. I waxed for the prevailing conditions and slipped into my bindings. I slipped the straps of my poles on my wrists and set off at a heart-quickening tempo onto a trail that circled the post for some twenty miles.

The aroma of roasting turkey was still in my nostrils as I glided the first five miles through lightly wooded terrain. Near the foothills of the mountains, I slowed to a more sedate pace, better suited to the fifteen miles or so I decided would be a good predinner workout for me today.

I settled into a solid, mile-eating rhythm and was lulled nearly to somnolence by the sound of the snow swishing against my skis. Hoar frost built up on my face and on the lenses of my goggles.

I continued climbing toward the base of the mountains. My pace slowed as the open woods gave way to thicker brush. After an hour, I stopped to drink from my OJ bottle and to take a short breather.

The forest was wrapped in winter silence. No birds were about. As my breathing subsided, I looked around at the snow-covered trees. It was beautiful, and oh, so peaceful here in the woods. I thought about bears then laughed out loud as I remembered all the bears were asleep now, deep in hibernation. Still, the hairs were standing up on the back of my neck. I was being observed.

Looking around, I spotted a small dog. It stood absolutely still, not moving, except for its tongue hanging and moving up and down with each breath, which floated visibly on the chilled air. Its eyes were locked with mine in an expression I found unsettling and strangely foreboding. Immediately, I thought of Bummer and wished I'd insisted he come along.

I dropped to one knee, still on my skis, and called to the dog. Standing in my path, it wasn't inherently threatening. However, nothing about the dog spoke of connection with humans. This seemed unnatural in a canine and more than a little sinister. Its tail was held rigid. It appeared to be studying me.

Spooked now, I decided to head for home. I wished that Bummer was with me. Swiveling on my skies, I swung my head to keep my eyes on the dog. It stood, silently regarding me.

I set off at a pace that would soon tire me. I slowed down into a rhythm I knew I could maintain indefinitely. Mounting a low summit, I raced down the other side.

I glanced over my shoulder to discover the dog was keeping pace with me. Only now he was joined by another larger and more wolf-like dog.

Startled by this new and more threatening pursuer, I crossed my tips and nearly fell. Pitching forward, I managed to catch my balance. Instinctively, I knew that to fall would bring more danger.

I stopped and turned my upper body so I faced the dogs. They were closer now. They approached to within a few yards and stood quietly, intimidating me.

My inclination, because I am at heart a dog lover, was to call to them. I knew instinctively they would not respond. I turned forward and moved on. *Bummer, my buddy, where are you?* I spotted, in my peripheral vision, a third dog moving up to join what was rapidly becoming a hunting pack of feral dogs. I really regretted now not having Bummer with me. He could easily handle three dogs.

Understanding now that I was in danger of my life, I begin skiing swiftly toward the post. I was on the edge of panic. I knew I needed to slow my pace or risk a fall.

I glanced to the rear. The dogs were keeping pace with me.

They moved silently, like wraiths through the trees, their silence more fearsome than would be their barking or howling.

I saw there were six of them, spread out in a semicircle, and closing on me.

Winded, I leaned on a tree to rest and gather myself.

Looking back, now there were seven of them quietly watching me. They were closer than before.

I grew angry. At the same time, I was thankful Bummer had stayed at home. He'd not be afraid to tangle with this gang of dogs, but seven was far too many for him to handle.

I swung a ski pole through the air and shouted, "Get outa' here. I'll break your necks! Shoo! Git!"

They comprised several different crossbreeds, some big and some not so big. Together, they pose a formidable threat if they decided to be unfriendly.

They didn't move. As one, they stood and stared me down, their tongues lolling and their lower jaws hanging open, revealing their fangs. They joined in a silent sinister phalanx.

Now I was really, really scared. I tried to think about how far I needed to go to reach the cantonment area of the post. It couldn't be far.

I shouted desperately, "Hello! Anybody there? Hey! Help!"

My cries were muffled by the snow-covered trees.

I felt foolish calling for help, threatened by a few dogs.

No one answered.

I studied the dogs.

They studied me.

I knew my only defense was to flee.

I skied as fast as I could down the trail whence I had come, caught a ski tip in a bush, and sprawled on my belly.

The pack closed in.

They were snarling and growling now as they circled me. I rolled onto my knees and waved my poles about as weapons, trying to keep them at bay.

The largest of them, the wolfish-looking dog, swept in, striking for my throat. Using a ski pole like an epee against his fangs, I fended him off, aiming at his eyes.

With a menacing growl, he backed off and gathered himself for another lunge.

I knew I had to get to my feet or I would surely be dog food at the end of day.

Gathering my strength, I faced the fiercest of the dogs and, teeth bared, growled my best ranger growl. At the same time, I waved my ski poles through the air.

The dogs backed away a few paces. I quickly got my hands under me and pushed myself upward. I had only one chance and was done for if I faltered.

I made it. The dogs backed still more and grew suddenly silent. They stood watching, waiting for me to fall.

I began to ski. I moved slowly, methodically, so as to be sure I did not lose my footing.

The dogs followed, now at a respectful distance, as we entered the housing area.

I recognized the back of my own house.

I stopped and looked back.

The dogs were gone.

The woods were silent. Snow was starting to fall.

I smelled the turkey cooking inside the house. I was alive and safe. I kicked off my skis and entered the safety of my own home.

My wife hugged me and said, "We were worried that you might be late for dinner."

Bummer, sensing my fading fear, sat attentively at my feet, looking up at me, letting me know in his own way he loved me. He sniffed inquisitively at my pant legs and growled softly.

I sat at table, joined hands with my family, and asked God's blessing of the meal.

Silently, I thanked God for giving me the strength to save myself from the feral dogs. I never shared this adventure with Brenda or the kids. I didn't want them to worry.

Of the many encounters I have had with the wild creatures that inhabit Alaska, none had been as sinister or menacing as this chance encounter with dogs gone wild. I vowed never to be caught so alone and helpless again without my dog.

The years went by too quickly. In 1979, I was promoted to lieutenant colonel and expected to be reassigned to Fort Monroe, Virginia. I dreaded it. My entire family, including Bummer, was acclimated to the northwestern environment. We'd lived in Washington and Alaska for a total of nine years now, with only the one-year break at Fort Leavenworth. None of us looked forward to moving east.

I asked for and was refused an additional year's extension at Fort Richardson. I was given three options: the Recruiting Command Headquarters at Fort Sheridan, Illinois; TRADOC Headquarters at

Fort Monroe; or the position as senior advisor to a reserve infantry brigade at Fort Snelling, Minnesota.

The commanding general of Alaskan Army Forces, Major General Ted Jenes, called for me. One of my duties as commander, combat developments activity (Alaska) was to advise the general on matters pertaining to the conduct of warfare in the extreme cold of the north. I had a lot of experience regarding that subject and had written field manuals and my master's thesis on fighting in the snow.

"Dick, what are your chances for extending here another year. We really need your expertise in this command."

"Slim to none, sir. I already tried, but Department of the Army denied my request and gave me three options. I like none of them," I explained what the options were.

"That brigade in Minneapolis is our designated 'round out' unit with orders to reinforce the Alaskan Brigade in the event of a Soviet incursion onto the mainland of Alaska. They've never been able to pass a readiness inspection for winter operations. You could do the Army a great service by taking the advisor assignment and bringing that reserve brigade up to snuff.

"Right now, it sounds like my best option if I want to remain with troops. I'll have to talk it over with Brenda, of course."

For several days, I discussed the pluses and minuses of our options with the family. In the end, Illinois was definitely out, and Fort Monroe seemed like another planet. We all agreed that Minnesota would be the best choice for the family, including Bummer.

16

In mid-September 1979, we started south on the Alcan Highway. We expected to see snow, what Alaskans call "termination dust," on a daily basis. The nights were below freezing. We had decided to pull the trailer along and live in it until we found a house in Minneapolis. There were no living quarters at Fort Snelling, so we'd have to find a house big enough for four and the dog. Evelyn, our younger daughter, had elected to stay in Anchorage.

Cindy, our older daughter, had graduated from high school in Kansas. She had come back to Alaska with us to work for the Red Cross. She decided to accompany us outside. She had her own car and would drive it down. Once more, we were in caravan mode.

Bummer had grayed around the muzzle and was aging not gracefully. He still acted and reacted to his environment as the "alpha dog" except when I was around. His inner coat filled out and thickened up with the approaching winter, and he looked to be the appropriate size for a malamute.

Our plan was to follow the Alcan to Mile One at Dawson Creek, Yukon, and proceed eastward along the main Canadian Highway until we reached Saskatoon, Saskatchewan (I had always wanted to go to Saskatoon. Why, I couldn't say). From there, we'd drop down into North Dakota and thence to Minnesota. I prayed we would not have an early winter, though we were certainly prepared for it.

We travelled down the Alcan, unpaved and extremely rough as the ground froze at the end of summer and before snow. We saw little traffic and each night camped in near-deserted campgrounds. We were glad to be able to let Bummer roam free and hunt for small critters. In southern Yukon, we had an inch of new snow. Bummer acted like it was Christmas.

We reached Minneapolis in good time and put up in the trailer park. Bummer's world suddenly diminished to walks on a leash. The few challengers he saw on his walks were subdued by a low growl. The next-door neighbor had a yappy little dog that seemed to resent Bummer's presence. When Bummer would respond with a growl and perhaps show his fangs, the little dog would run yelping to his owner. When the neighbor complained, I told her to mind her dog and that was the end of it.

We found rentals very costly and unsuitable to our liking so began looking to buy. We found a beautiful home on an acre of land in Apple Valley to the south of the city. Its cost was more than we could afford on lieutenant colonel's pay, but Brenda dearly loved the house and agreed to go to work to help with the payments.

I spent some time during the first days walking the dog along the boundaries of the Apple Valley property, letting him mark his territory, knowing he would not stray beyond the limits we set together. He was a house dog now.

Our acre consisted of several dead oak trees among many living adult specimens, and I spent the first autumn cutting enough firewood to last us the three winters we expected to be here. Bummer spent the time hunting squirrels and celebrating each time he made a kill.

We spent many winter's evenings before the great brick fireplace watching television together as a family. Bummer stretched out before the fire hoping for a belly scratch now and then. We each loved him in our way and wished he could be with us forever, but he was growing older.

Brenda spent three days away from home each week working for a real-estate brokerage. Bummer had some alone time in the house. He seemed all right with that but demanded maximum attention and loving in the evenings. He missed his breakfast conversations with the mother.

The family members continued to grow and change. Cindy married and went back to Alaska to be with her soldier husband. Evelyn came home and later went back to Alaska. They say once you experience Alaska, you never can go all the way back outside.

There were just us four now: Brenda and me, Chris, who was about to graduate from high school, and Bummer. Brenda elected to go to work full time. This meant the dog spent long hours alone in the house. My duties took me away to neighboring cities and states for many evenings and overnights.

The winter of 1980 bought heavy snows. We were able to ski off the roof top. Chris skied for the Buck Hill Ski Team. I had visions of his making the U.S. Olympic Alpine Team. He was that good. Bummer hunted varmints in the deep snow. He loved it. It was clear to me he loved Chris too. Chris loved him as well. They spent a lot of time together.

At night, I'd sit on the floor with the dog in front of the fireplace. Sometimes, he'd talk to me in growls and yelps like he once had done with Brenda at the breakfast table. These conversations were like, "I love you as much as a dog can love. I wish I could be with you always." I scratched behind his ears and rubbed his belly and his whole body, trying to let him know I loved him too.

Winter ended. Chris was to graduate from high school that year. He and I visited with his ski coach in the spring.

"Coach, what do you see as Chris's chances for making the Olympic team this year?"

"Can't see it. He excels in downhill. He's the best on the team. But he needs more work in slalom. He should have one more year of prep. Next year, he may make the Junior Olympics. We'll see."

I met alone later with Chris.

"I'm willing to sponsor you for one more year on the Buck Hill Team. But these are the conditions. You will ski, and that's all you will do, summer and winter. I'll send you to ski racing camp this summer at Mount Hood, Oregon, and to Alaska when we run out of snow. You'll have to work hard to make the team."

When Chris said nothing, I continued, "It's okay, you got a couple of months before you graduate. Think it over, and let me know what you want to do."

Chris came to me about a month later. "I wanted only to be the best. The room at the top of the skiing profession is very narrow. I choose not to continue with my ski racing efforts."

"That's okay, son. I would rather you go to college anyway."

"I'm not really ready for college either."

"Well, you got about a month to decide, but I'll tell you one thing. You're not gonna lay around the house all day watching television."

I didn't know Chris had opted to enlist in the military until he came to me one day and told me he wanted to join the marines and could I look at his papers and see if the recruiter was telling the truth. I looked over the documents and called the sergeant to ask him some questions.

"The offer looks good to me," I said to Chris. "You're guaranteed a slot in Marine Aviation Electronics. If that's what you want to do, I'd say go for it."

Chris left for boot camp in San Diego. And then there were three.

Bummer missed him a great deal. He grew feeble and lost bladder control. He began to urinate daily on the rug in the hallway. We decided he'd have to be kept outside. I built a dog run with an entrance into the garage. While we continued to enjoy evenings in front of the fire, at night and each following day, Bummer was exiled to the garage and a small external run.

The winter of 1983 brought extreme cold without the blanketing warmth of snow. The Bummer felt the effects of the cold as well as the loneliness of his enforced solitude. At the same time, I was trying to rebound from the effects of a career gone sour and health gone south. My years in Vietnam had caught up with me. I underwent major surgery and resection of my large and small intestines. I healed slowly. Brenda continued to work full time and try to keep the household together. Cindy had moved to North Dakota with her husband. Chris was gone overseas with the Marines. Evelyn was in Alaska. The Bummer was slowly dying in his pen.

The winter went on and on. We burned a lot of oak in the fireplace. We longed for the insulating qualities of snow cover. There were evenings we'd invite the dog inside to share the fire with us. My poor Bummer—I loved him so much, I hated to see him lose his faculties. He'd lay on the floor beside me, panting for breath, and lick my hand when I offered it. I suspected his vision was growing dim. When the evenings were over, I hated having to once more confine him alone in the freezing cold garage. We thought it time to put him to sleep.

When spring finally came, Bummer's spirits seemed to pick up. Summer came on hot. Bummer once again lost energy. His coat came away in patches. Once again, we considered taking him on one final trip to the vet. Chris was due home on furlough from the Marines, and we were determined to give the dog one last sight of the boy he loved. Conversely, we knew Chris dearly loved the dog and would want to see him for one final time.

We had made the final decision. On the following afternoon, I came home from Fort Snelling and went to let Bummer out of his run. I had just stepped out the back door when my eye was caught by sudden movement. The dog leapt into the lower branches of the one tree growing in the dog run and caught a gray squirrel.

For the moment, he seemed his old self as he ran to meet me with his proud "in your face" attitude. I dropped on one knee, hugged him close, and said, "Oh, Bummer. You are The Bummer. You're my main dog." I scratched behind his ears, and he licked my face. I didn't mind. We had a reprieve from the inevitable. Bummer objected, however, when I gave the squirrel a decent burial with honors.

Chris came home, and we had a fine reunion dinner—a porterhouse steak for Chris and a whole silver salmon for Bummer. Then Chris was gone, and we faced Bummer's relapse into old age.

I called the vet and told him I was bringing in a dog that needed to be put to sleep. The next day, I cancelled the appointment. I couldn't face the death of my fishing partner. But there were no fishing trips left for my faithful dog. I called back and reset the appointment with the vet.

The day—it was that day I had to lift the dog into the back of my suburban. Thoughts of the Alcan and The Bummer hopping out and then back into the back of our Blazer ran through my mind. As I lifted him, arms around the front of his forelegs and around the back of his hind legs, he looked at me with gratitude in his eyes as if he understood what was coming. I laid him down in the back of the

Chevy. He whined in sudden pain and then licked my cheek as if in gratitude for what we were about.

Our trip to the vet was fairly short yet one of the longest trips I had ever taken. I prayed God to keep this dog's soul in heaven to await our arrival. I remembered all the lifetime experiences I had been privileged to share with this dog. My eyes misted, and I continued driving with some difficulty.

Arriving at the animal hospital, I parked and went inside alone to see what I was supposed to do. I paid the bill in advance because I knew I'd be in no condition to pay later.

I went out to get my dog. He lay where I had placed him in the back of the suburban. I lifted him up gently and held him in my arms. How light he felt compared to what he had been. I walked back into the hospital and placed him on a steel table, all the while hugging him close. The vet approached wielding a long needle. He seemed unaffected by this momentous occasion. I hugged Bummer closer. He looked at me as if in gratitude. He died looking deeply into my eyes. I felt his muscles tense and then go slack as his eyes glazed over. He was dead—dead. He relaxed totally and died in my arms.

I felt or heard a high-pitched wail, and I thought it must be coming from Bummer. Then I realized the scream was coming from me. My own eyes glazed over with tears. I howled in pain for my dog. At that moment, I wanted to die with him. The wild spirit of the exceptional animal had flown. I prayed his soul was with God. I wanted to know I would see him again someday in heaven. If he wasn't there waiting for me, what I felt was the sense in my going. My Catholic sensibility told me neither the Catechism nor the Bible said anything about the souls of dogs, but I needed to believe Bummer would be waiting for us in heaven.

I dropped his now limp body on the steel table and fled, bawling like a baby, my eyes streaming tears for my canine companion, my dead dog, my beloved companion.

I can't remember the drive home or how I managed to keep from colliding with another vehicle. I only remember putting the car in the now empty garage and pulling myself together to face Brenda.

We both cried as she insisted I give her a step-by-step description of how Bummer died. We both vowed we would never have another dog. How could any dog replace The Bummer?

If we were to lose a son or a daughter, when our mother and father die, do we seek to get a replacement? No. The dead can only be missed and remembered. They add depth and beauty to our human experience. Our dog had been a vital member of our family for fourteen years, most of the lifetimes of our children. He could not be replaced—only mourned and missed.

Years later, Evelyn wrote of her continuing feelings about Bummer.

Memoir to My Best Friend
I don't think anybody knew this.
He was my best friend,
my confidant.

I immediately loved him.
He was wild like my soul.

He was everything I wanted to be.
I admired him,
and he, me.

His unspoken words,
just a glance,
a look—
that's all it took.

17

We mourned Bummer for more than a year. The house in Apple Valley just wasn't the same without him. Brenda and I discussed getting a new dog but agreed no dog could replace our Bummer.

This was supposed to be my last station. I'd make twenty years and be eligible to retire before my tour was up. But everything went sour when my boss retired and was replaced by a two-star general, a mean man who didn't agree with my mission to train the brigade to fight in the snow. My old boss was replaced with a colonel who was a creature of the general's making. His job was to make me tow the mark with the general's policies or get rid of me.

Brenda agreed I could not retire under these shameful conditions. I called on my old friends in the "Airborne Mafia" who would be stationed at Fort Bragg, North Carolina, with the Eighty-Second Airborne Division and the Eighteenth Airborne Corps and wangled a tour on the general staff at corps. I knew it would be my last and vowed to myself I would give it my best shot.

I came away, decorated for my efforts at corps, and retired in 1985 with highest honors. Now I could rest on my laurels.

We headed for Tacoma to reclaim our house in Lakewood. I never thought of getting another dog. We refurbished our house in Tacoma and settled in. Memories of Bummer flooded in, but they were mellowed now from the dark days preceding his death. Nowadays, when I think of Minnesota, that's all I remember. But now I could recall the dog in his burgeoning into the prime of life. It was enough. When I thought of him, I was reminded of Snake and Little Joe. I thanked God for affording me the privilege of knowing and sharing life with these extraordinary creatures.

With the house finished and the two of us moved in for fair, we settled down to live in retirement. The memories of Bummer slowly faded in our memories. We talked sometimes about getting another "pet" but decided we didn't want one until one day we were visited by the mallards.

"Dick, come out here quick," my wife Brenda called to me from the patio. I was just finishing my second cup of coffee. The outside door from the kitchen was open. It was a lovely June morning, rare in the Pacific Northwest.

"What's the matter?" I asked, starting up and heading for the door.

"I think there's a duck on the roof," she said. I slowed a bit with the knowledge that all Lakewood wasn't burning down. I smiled as I thought of the beginnings of a poem: *Dick, come quick! I think there's a duck on*—well, maybe just a limerick.

I stepped out onto the patio and looked up where Brenda was looking, and sure enough, there on the shakes stood a pretty female mallard.

Nervously, she looked us over. "Quack," she said.

"Let's go inside. Maybe she'll come down," Brenda said.

"By all means," I said, as we moved toward the door.

Brenda loved all birds. Our house, wherever it might be, was always a bird sanctuary. Lord, help the cat who came bird hunting around our place.

After a bit, sure enough, the duck flew to the patio floor. She looked about and gave a couple of satisfied chortles, which sounded amazingly like, "Quack, quack."

Then she waddled straight for the door.

"I'll get a slice of bread. Maybe she'll eat it," said Brenda excitedly. "Maybe I should get some water too." Not many things excited Brenda, but the presence of birds was one of them.

After eating some of the bread, Suzie, as my wife immediately named her, took a few sips of water. Then she flew away toward a nearby pond.

The next day, she was back. We observed pretty much the same scenario.

On the third day, she came again. This time, she had a beautiful mallard drake in tow. Brenda immediately dubbed him "Sammy."

We, my wife Brenda and I, spent summer afternoons lounging in our very private backyard at a house we owned in the Lakewood suburb of Tacoma, Washington. I had bricked in the patio and planted rhododendrons to augment the mountain laurels and the several mature Douglas firs that surrounded the house. The evergreen shrubbery was reinforced by platoons of flowers. It was a very private place. It was our quiet place until that day when we began sharing it with Suzie and Sammy.

Suzie, she who was to be obeyed, took immediate possession of the lawn, waddling about on what was to become her daily inspection tour, bobbling her head to and fro, and occasionally giving orders to Sammy.

"M-mrack, ckk, ckk," she'd say.

Sammy—resplendent in his iridescent green, blue, and white mating plumage—responded with a dip of his beak and "R-r-r-uck, ruck" as he followed her about, being careful to remain positioned between his lovely mate and us, protecting her from possible harm.

Brenda and I wondered why they picked this place to land. We discussed it *ad nauseum*, during the remainder of the summer we shared with the pair of mallards. They returned again on the second day, and when they returned on the third day, we noticed Sammy was a good flyer, totally in control during landings. He usually flared into a stall just as his feet touched down. Most often, he made it a three-point landing by skidding to a stop on his derriere.

Suzie, on the other hand, tended to come in too hot, skidding on her belly, and twice out of three attempts, spinning head over teakettle on the grass.

On the third day, we noticed that Suzie had picked up a splinter, a big one, in her left foot. To say that it was a splinter is an understatement. It was more like a straw-colored twig that extended from somewhere in the center of her foot to beyond the webbing between her toes. She presented herself as the legendary lame duck incarnate.

Thenceforth, each evening, shortly after sundown, Suzie would commence her departure ritual. She waddled toward the front yard and then skittered sideways in both directions a few feet. Sammy followed a pace or two to the rear. Both ducks sounded off with an authoritative "qua-a-ack, quack."

When Suzie had her take-off line properly set up between the trees, she'd waggle her head at Sammy, and off they'd go, heading, we presumed for one of the two small lakes that lay close by our home.

We wondered if they were raising a family at lakeside and retreated to our house for a midafternoon break from parenting.

That night, our pillow talk focused on the mallard pair. Brenda said, "Suzie has got to be in a lot of pain because of that foot."

"Yes. I wonder if that's why she makes such bad landings or if her lack of landing skill was the cause of her problem. At any rate, she had probably tried to land among some rushes and picked up the splinter in the process."

"Can't we do something for her?"

"If they come back tomorrow, I'll try to catch her and pull the splinter out."

"Maybe," Brenda said, "we should try to make some kind of pond for them."

Wide awake now, I could see this was quickly becoming a second career for me. I imagined the "angel of worries" looking down on us and thinking, *Aha, there's Dick, recently retired from Army service and just finished remodeling his house. Kids all grown up and flown the nest. He thinks he hasn't got a worry in the world. I'll just show him it doesn't work that way for the living. The mallard family needs a little help.*

The next morning, I hunted around in the garage and found my salmon net and an old, unused dishpan. I pounded out the bigger dents. I dug a hole in the backyard and sank the pan in it to provide a reasonable facsimile of the ol' swimmin' hole for Mister and Missus Mallard. Satisfied it would serve, I filled it with fresh water.

That afternoon, Brenda and I waited impatiently for the ducks to arrive. I watered the lawn attempting to literally grease the skids for landing. Brenda stood by with antiseptic and bandages. I fingered my salmon net with which I planned to capture Suzie.

They showed at the scheduled time, Suzie in the lead as usual. She made her approach at warp speed and settled onto the lawn like an F-4 making a crosswind landing on an aircraft carrier. She skidded to a stop on her belly.

After Sammy glided to a perfect stop, she began limping about, looking for something to eat in the grass. We noticed that her gait had worsened.

We swung into action. Brenda circled to the left, arms spread wide. I circled to the right. Suzie retreated under a bush. Sammy observed the action calmly from under a lawn chair. Suzie started quacking.

On the third try, I managed to get the net over Suzie. I planted its metal hoop firmly on the ground and scooped her up. Feathers flew. Brenda managed to get both her hands on Suzie's body. She hugged the duck close, trying not to hurt her.

I threw the net aside and, as Brenda held her, took her left foot firmly in my left hand, and with my right fingers, deftly extracted the splinter. I say deftly. Actually, it came out with ease.

Suzie immediately stopped squirming and quacking. She lay quietly in Brenda's hands. Brenda handed her to me and began to wash the duck's appendage with antiseptic. She inspected the foot for any remaining splinters and wrapped it with waterproof tape.

Placed back on the turf, Suzie calmly walked to the dish-pan-cum-swimming pool, plopped into it, and began swimming around contentedly. Sammy waddled over to join her. I imagined the angel of worries, as he or she or whatever, placed gold stars on our service records.

The mallards made our backyard their summer palace for the rest of that warm season. We accepted them as part of our family and looked forward each day to their arrival.

The normal drill was for Brenda and me to sit relaxing on the patio enjoying a cooling drink until Suzie and Sammy arrived. They'd land (Suzie's landing skill had improved somewhat) and walk about for a while. Then she'd pop into the pool for a quick dunk before the two of them settled under a bush and roosted until late afternoon when it was time for their departure.

When the weather turned hot, they spent hours nesting under the laurels in our backyard. As the weeks went by, they began ranging outward from our yard into the streets in search of whatever it was she was looking for. It must have been food, but I couldn't for the life of me figure out what it was she was finding to eat in the gutters along the road.

We lived on a corner lot. A through street ran along one side of our house and crossed a cul-de-sac that ran in front of the house. As Suzie ranged up and down the streets, scouring the bottoms of the roadside ditches, Sammy rode shotgun along the edges of the tarmac, keeping careful watch over his comely bride.

We worried about their safety, especially on the busier through street. I tried to keep them on the cul-de-sac where there was hardly any traffic. When I spotted Sammy on the wrong road, I'd herd them both back onto the cul-de-sac and the front of the house.

One day, I was working in the front yard while Suzie was working the gutters, when a car passed at a fairly high rate of speed. I heard one of the ducks give a loud squawk. Looking up, I saw a cloud of feathers flying near the edge of the road. Hurrying over, I found Sammy's broken body in the ditch.

The car was nowhere to be seen. Neither was Suzie.

Gathering up poor Sammy, I saw he was still alive but with one wing hanging limply and one of his thighs shattered. There was no telling what injuries he sustained internally. Tears clouded my eyes as I carried him carefully into the backyard and placed him under a laurel bush to die.

I knew he had to be in great pain. I hoped he would die quickly.

Brenda and I waited for Suzie to come back, but she never returned that day.

The next morning, when I got out of bed, I quickly dressed and went out to see to Sammy. He hadn't moved from the position in which I placed him. Unfortunately, he was still alive. There was nothing to do but put him quickly out of his misery. I tearfully, prayerfully dispatched him and buried him in the yard.

We mourned him the rest of the summer.

At the beginning of fall, Suzie returned with a new partner. Her foot was totally healed, but her landings hadn't improved very much.

We welcomed her and tolerated her new beau, but we couldn't bear to name him. Things just could never be quite the same.

After a few days, the ducks disappeared, probably to fly south for the winter. We never saw Suzie again.

Now whenever we see mallards, we think of the ducks that enriched our lives for a summer by sharing theirs with us. All these years, Suzie and Sammy have remained in our hearts as part of our family. Whenever Brenda sees mallards flying overhead, she points to them and says ritually, "There go Suzie and Sammy."

18

The ducks were cute and loveable, but they carried with them a heartrending vulnerability. We shared a summer with them, but they offered nothing of their wild ways that said I want to share my life with you. We needed a dog.

I had finished with improvement projects on my house and was growing bored. I continued my running discipline from army days and looked forward to skiing, but it wasn't enough. An acquaintance told me about a government project they were working on at Fort Lewis. They were hiring retired officers, and I applied for an interview. I didn't really understand what the project was about, but since I had graduate systems management courses from USC, I decided to hire on and learn as I went. It turned out to be a bad job. I never really knew what we were trying to accomplish, but one of the men I worked with, Larry Collings, owned an AKC registered German shepherd who had just given birth to a litter of puppies. He invited me over to see them. One afternoon, I followed him home from work.

As I entered the driveway, I was greeted by a handsome female German shepherd. Her name was Tacoma. She raced over to the car and welcomed me to her home. I took this as a good sign. She appeared anxious to show off her new brood, ten little puppies barely able to see.

Larry showed me into the mudroom at the back of his house, and there, huddled in a cardboard box, were the puppies. Only the word *puppies* could describe the little black balls of fur with black eyes searching this brand new world about them. They would have weighed in at little more than a pound apiece. I picked one up and looked into its eyes. It couldn't see yet but tried to suckle one of my fingers.

As Tacoma entered the mudroom, the pups scrambled to suckle as she lay down for them in the cardboard box. I noticed one pup, who had left the box on his own, met his mother head on and licked her on the nose. He continued to investigate the room as Tacoma began feeding the others. I thought perhaps he had lost his way, but then he approached his mother and, pushing the other pups aside, began to feed. He finished his meal and strutted about, continued to explore. I stooped and picked him up. He squirmed to be free and then settled down to study my face. I held him close to study him, and he licked my nose, smiling as if to say, "Gotcha."

Larry, seeing I was captivated by this dog, tied a blue ribbon loosely around his neck.

"Yeah, I want him, Larry, but you understand—he has to pass muster with my wife. We had agreed we wouldn't have another dog just yet."

"Sure. I'll keep the ribbon on this pup until you bring your wife over to see him. Once she seen the puppy, I'm sure she'll want him as much as you do."

I drove home wondering how I could get Brenda to agree to see the pups.

"You're late. Supper is ready. Did you stop somewhere?"

We sat together and asked the blessing before I answered, mental fingers crossed, "I stopped off at Larry Collings's house. You remember my speaking about him? His German shepherd just had a litter of pups, and he wanted me to see them."

"Oh?"

"Yeah, you oughta see them. She's had ten, and they are so cute. Their eyes are just opening."

"Dick, I know where you're going with this. You know what we agreed."

"I know—I know. But won't you please agree to go over just to see them?"

She didn't answer for some time.

"Boy, is this spaghetti ever good," I said. "You sure know how to cook it, better than anybody."

"Oh, all right. I'll go look at the pups—but just to look. Agreed?"

"Agreed."

I left the table to call Larry and tell him we were on our way over to see the pups.

We arrived to find Tacoma feeding her pups in the mudroom. I held back as Brenda studied each of the pups. Nine of them were struggling among themselves to get their mother's attention. One roamed the room by itself, sniffing out the corners, investigating everything. Around its neck was a blue ribbon. Brenda stooped and picked the pup up. She studied him as he studied her. He licked her nose.

"This is the one," she said.

"This is the one, what?"

"This is our new dog." She looked at me, a knowing smile on her face.

And so it was decided. The pups would not be weaned and ready for adoption for another month. I visited the brood every day after work. Each day, Tacoma would greet me like a new son in law and escort me to the mudroom. The pups would rush to their dame, expecting a meal. Our pup would greet his mom with a lick on the nose and then rush to greet me, hoping at first and then demanding to be picked up and cuddled. He was soon able to see. He'd look at me with coal black eyes that promised we'd be best of friends, tail flailing like a banner.

At around eight weeks old, Tacoma decided her pups were ready to join their new human families. One day at work, Larry told me my dog was ready to go home with me. At the end of the day, I rushed to his house, anxious to claim the new member of my family, at first a black and later mostly black-, brown-, and silver-tipped AKC pedigreed German shepherd.

We started for home together. I deposited him on the front seat of our now venerable Chevy suburban beside me for the short drive home. He moved around the truck sniffing at every newly discovered corner of the vehicle. His exploratory expedition completed, he sat down on the front seat and vomited. He would require some adaptation to his new environment.

"Brenda, we're home." I set the pup on the living room floor.

Brenda rushed in from the kitchen, wiping her hands on a dish towel. She stopped when she saw the dog sitting straddle-legged on the floor, his head hanging.

"What's the matter with him?"

"He got car sick in the Chev. He'll be all right pretty soon."

She drew a bowl of water and set it on the kitchen floor. I placed the dog before it. He lapped at it noisily, sharing it with the kitchen floor. Then he sat down on the linoleum, looked up at me, looked at Brenda, belched once, and set about exploring his new home.

I followed him about, watching for signs that he was about to relieve himself. We'd learned this drill while housebreaking Bummer. We'd placed newspapers on the laundry room floor. At the first sign of a squat, I picked him up with a gentle "No, no" and moved quickly to place him on the newspapers where he promptly rewarded me with a piddle or a pile. I praised him and rewarded him with a bit of dog biscuit.

That evening, we set a fire in the fireplace, and I settled in my leather recliner, the pup sleeping on my lap. Brenda sat in her favorite chair beside me.

"What are we going to name him?"

"Well, AKC registration requires at least three names. His father's name was Grand Misty's Proud Smokey, and his mother's name is Clayfield Tacoma Collings. He prances around the house like he owns the world like a maharaja. I think we ought to include something of both his dame's and his sire's legal names in his title, say, Tacoma's Proud Maharaja. What do you think of that?"

"Sounds good, but we can't go around calling him all that."

"No, we'll call him Rajah or just Raj for short."

After three days, we began to move him outside whenever he gave signs that he needed to go. After a week, he was totally housebroken and whined at the door whenever he needed to go.

During the first week, we attempted to confine him to the kitchen and laundry room by blocking the two doors leading out of the kitchen with baby gates. He was okay with that as long as one of us was in the kitchen, but in the evening when we relaxed in the living room, he cried and jumped at the gate until we gave in and let him join us. We finally gave up the gates as a failed idea.

Rajah developed the habit of spending evenings in my lap. I'd keep my legs together, and he'd settle belly up in the crease between my legs, his head on one of my knees, legs displayed akimbo in the air like a discarded TV antenna. Tongue hanging between sharp puppy teeth, he'd go fast asleep as I rubbed his belly. I wondered what we'd do when he outgrew my lap.

I wanted to begin taking Rajah along with me in the Chev, but he had a tendency to get car sick, so each day, I took him on a short trip around the neighborhood, extending the distance daily until after a couple of weeks, he became inured to motion sickness. He came to love riding shotgun in the suburban, keeping a sharp eye out for dangerous squirrels.

Brenda appreciated the break. When left at home, Raj would be continually underfoot and would often nip at her ankles with those sharp puppy teeth until her lower legs were streaked with scratches and cuts. Fortunately, he quickly grew beyond this habit.

The old saying, "It's easier to take the man out of the Army than the Army out of the man." held true with me. I ran a couple of miles each day to keep myself fit. I started taking The Raj along, slowly at first and mindful of his puppy legs and feet. I attached a leash to his collar and held it short and led him on my left side. After a few fits and starts and several tumbles over the leash, he got the hang of it. Soon, he ran without a leash, keeping his nose close to my left calf and later, as he grew to his full 120 pounds, my left thigh. He often glanced up at my face to catch signals of my intentions. I'd smile at him and rub the top of his head.

He grew to be a beautiful dog—the most beautiful shepherd I'd ever seen. He had a fine temperament and liked to strut around the house living up to his namesake. His coat was mostly black with patches of brown in all the right places for a German shepherd. His back and shoulders were sprinkled with silver highlights. His brow was black and highlighted with brown in such a way as to give him a deceptively peaceful expression, deceptive because he was aggressively curious about everything and everybody. Visitors found his literally in-your-face curiosity intimidating. He was at best indifferent to strangers. Once he'd had a close look and a smell or two, he'd usually ignore them, except for Rich Poelker, a boyhood friend of mine. For some reason, he didn't like Rich—never did. Rich always had to move slow and cautiously around The Raj.

The dog was different with children whom he universally loved. Kids could do anything with him, and he'd stand or lie calmly allowing them to climb all over him.

19

In early 1986, Chris came home after receiving an honorable discharge from the Marine Corps. He'd decided not to stay for a second hitch. He lived at home while attending college. Later, he moved into his own place and went to work at Boeing. Brenda and I were happy that at least one of our kids had chosen to live close to us. Cindy was married, had two girls, and ultimately moved to Houston, Texas. Evelyn chose to go back to Alaska.

When Rajah was nine months old, we decided he should attend obedience classes. Though he still had a lot of puppy in him, physically, he was full grown at 120 pounds. But where other dogs that size tended to be clumsy and push their weight around, Rajah was light on his feet and very agile. I was a little nervous because while The Raj wasn't hostile toward other dogs, he was aggressively curious, feared nothing, and was unlikely to back down from a fight. I had no idea how he'd react to a group of dogs.

We entered the classroom together on the first day of doggie school. We joined a dozen or so other dogs of various breeds and sizes accompanied by their nervous owners in a bare room about thirty by thirty feet. On one wall was a window-sized opening to the outside. The floor was bare boards. The only furnishings were just enough folding chairs to hold the owners who were present. The dogs were arrayed in various positions at their owners' feet. I was happy to see the dogs were all restrained. Rajah was only mildly interested in the other canine scholars and responded readily to urgings on his lead. When I sat at one end of the row of occupied chairs, he promptly sat at my left, his right shoulder in contact with my left calf.

The instructor, a woman, stood before us and conducted roll call, recognizing each dog in turn. I could tell by her attitude she favored the smaller dogs. She explained what the course of instruction would be and that the training was as much for the owner as for the dog. Rajah sat attentively as if taking mental notes.

The rest of the class consisted of a variety of dogs. There was a handsome beagle, a standard poodle, a Labrador retriever pup, and several mixed breeds. The Lab turned out to be the class clown.

Each week for the following eight weeks, we took turns putting our dogs through their paces. They learned to sit, stand, lie down, heel, and stay on command. We humans learned the importance of hand signals to supplement verbal commands.

Rajah loved this training and looked forward eagerly to every session. One evening, I was walking around the room performing an exercise with Rajah at the heel. I glanced down at him. His head was held high, and he was lifting his front feet like a Lipizzan show horse. He was prancing. I stopped, and dropping to one knee, I grasped his head with both hands and looked him straight in the eye. He looked back at me proudly and, smiling, seemed to say, "Aren't I smart? Aren't you proud of me?" I looked at him for another moment. My eyes teared. I knew he could sense my love for him and my pride in him. The moment over, I stood and we continued the exercise. I looked over at the instructor and was surprised to see a tear in her eye as well.

On the last day of training, the owners took turns putting our dogs through their paces. Ribbons were to be awarded for the best three dogs: blue for best, red for second best, and yellow for third. I was confident Rajah would take the blue. Only one exercise worried me: the dogs were ordered to sit and stay for three minutes while the owner walked away to the other side of the room, turned, and faced the sitting dog. The dog was required to sit for the three minutes without moving. At a signal the exercise was over, each dog was required to return directly to its owner on command.

Rajah performed each exercise flawlessly up to the one in which he was required to remain immobile for three minutes. I walked him to the designated spot, looked him straight in the eye, and ordered him to "sit" and pointed at the floor. With military precision, he dropped his rear end silently to the floor. I ordered him to stay and held up my hand, palm first in front of his nose. I turned my back to him, and marching to the other side of the room, I halted and faced about. I knew the sharper I made these movements, the better Rajah would perform.

Rajah sat, ears perked, watching me intently. He didn't move a muscle. I stood watching him, willing him not to move for what seemed a very long time. The Raj held steady and very much alert.

When the instructor signaled that the time was up, I commanded, "Rajah, come." He rose swiftly and, displaying that Lipizzan prance, bounded directly to me and sat smartly before me. I don't know which of us was the prouder. He looked up at me, tongue hanging between snow-white lower fangs. I looked down at him. Something passed between us that I knew neither of us would forget. We knew we had aced it together.

We performed the few remaining exercises flawlessly and sat down, drawing applause from the other dog owners.

The only dog that could possibly do better than The Raj was the beagle. He had demonstrated perfection during practice. I knew the instructor was biased toward small dogs. He had appeared on several occasions to be intimidated by Rajah as well as the Labrador retriever. The instructor was the sole judge of the dogs' performances.

The beagle executed every exercise crisply and prettily. I thought he might win over Rajah. His owner executed the drill requiring the dog to walk around the room at heel without a leash. Something must have caught the beagle's eye from out the window because like a shot, he leapt out and was gone.

Rajah was awarded his first and only blue ribbon. The instructor asked if she could take some measurements of the dog because she wanted to sign a contract with me to show him. We found Rajah perfect in all dimensions except he was at maximum height at the shoulders and his tail, nearly dragging on the ground, was maximum length for show.

"Let me know if you will agree to let me show him. His face, if nothing else, will win prizes for him. If you want to show him as a working dog, I will agree to train him and show him at no cost to you."

"Doesn't that mean he'd spend a lot of time away from home?"

"Yes, if he works out like I think he will."

"Thanks, but I can't do without him at home. Your offer is tempting, but Rajah is needed at home. Sorry."

"I understand. Let me know if you change your mind. This dog has a championship attitude."

When Rajah was about a year old, we decided to move to Vashon Island on Puget Sound where we had discovered, while helping retiring military friends to find a place to live, a beautiful waterfront home.

So in November 1986, we sold our Tacoma home and moved to Vashon Island. Soon thereafter, I took Rajah for a walk on the beach at low tide. He loved the freedom of it. He romped about on the sand with glee and then discovered a new and marvelous element—the sea. He entered at first tentatively then with increasing abandon into the saltwater. Stopping to drink of it, he looked at me quizzically as he tasted the saltiness in it.

I liked the beach too because it gave me a sense of freedom I hadn't felt before. I could let Rajah run free without fear of interfering humans. I always carried his lead with me in case people appeared not because I was afraid of what the dog might do but because I feared anyone encountering his great size, strength, and exuberance might be intimidated by him. I felt people had a right to be on the beach without fear or intimidation—not in my America. It was something I had fought for as a soldier.

Most of the time, we had the beach to ourselves. I bought a Frisbee and loved throwing it out into the surf for The Raj to retrieve. He loved running into the waves and often swimming out to get the disk and bring it back for me to throw again. At first, I was fearful of throwing it too far. Soon, I learned I couldn't throw it far enough. He'd brave very large waves to get to the Frisbee and, just before I began to panic, bring it back and drop it at my feet. He'd stop, look up at me with tongue hanging, smile, and want to go again. What fun we had! Those days were the best of many I shared with The Raj.

I decided I wanted to see what he could do on land, so I took him up to the electric company offices where they had around three acres of open grass field in front of the building with nobody around. I stopped the Chev near the front door of the offices and walked to the lawn accompanied by Rajah.

I had grown quite adept at throwing the Frisbee. As I prepared to let sail, Rajah, understanding my body language, stood to one side at the ready. I sailed it down the field as far as I could throw it. Rajah, legs grown strong from running in the surf, launched himself in pursuit of the disk and propelled himself a good six feet in the air to grasp it in his maw before running to bring it back for me to toss again. I was thrilled and overjoyed at his great skill. I got in the habit of taking him up to "our lawn" on an almost daily basis. When walkers by began gathering to watch the show, I stopped and went back to the beach and its solitude.

That year, my good friend from the Army, Phil McClure, moved in just a few houses down from me. His crazy dog, Dandy, had died before he left the Army, and he bought a new dog, a yellow Labrador pup. He asked me to go to Puyallup with him to pick up the new pup, and I agreed to ride along with him in his wife Joyce's new Buick sedan. We snarfed up the pup, a beautiful little male yellow Lab, and headed back to the island. I sat holding the dog in my lap. Before long, he appeared to suffer from motion sickness as Rajah had when I brought him home. Rather than have him make a mess on Joyce's new upholstery, I stuck the pup's nose into my jacket pocket and let him barf there. Phil decided to call the pup Dusty.

Soon, Dusty and Raj were playing on the beach and in the waves. We all had lots of fun. Dusty would run full out, trying to keep up with Rajah. In a few months, Dusty outweighed Rajah and was able to best him in the water. They'd both go out after a well-thrown Frisbee and wrestle for it. Dusty would step on Rajah and push him under water. Game over.

Rajah loved to run on the beach in daylight or dark. Often, I went clamming at night because the low tides occurred late those years. The dog went with me and ran through the water as I dug.

One night, we were returning together with a mess of butter clams when Rajah suddenly took off running. I aimed my flashlight ahead of his sprinting body and saw the eyes of two large raccoons reflected in the light. I dropped the clams and ran calling Rajah as loud as I could. Those coons could not frighten my big shepherd, but they could surely make a mess out of him if he cornered them. They managed to reach the shore ahead of Rajah and disappeared into the woods.

Rajah ranged back and forth looking for a scent and then returned fully winded to my side. I checked him out for wounds and, when I found none, walked back and retrieved my sack full of clams.

One day, we walked together down the beach near high tide. It was a typically cloudy day with little wind on Puget Sound. As we walked together along the beach, we passed under the branches of a maple tree that leaned toward the water. Just then, Rajah alerted and began to circle. A white feather floated down out of the tree and landed on the sand. Rajah ran over to it and began sniffing at it. Again, he began circling. I looked up and, on the branch above our heads, sat a bald eagle pecking at the carcass of a gull.

I sat down on a driftwood log and watched the eagle feed. It was maybe fifteen feet above us but never paid any attention to me or my dog. Rajah continued to circle and search for the source of the scent he smelt, but he never thought to look up.

Finally finishing its meal, the eagle spread its magnificent wings and soared seaward. Eagles—one; gulls—nothing. I'd had a front row seat at the show put on by the eagle and laughed at Rajah who had been made to look the fool.

In November 1997, I applied for and was hired for a new job as in medical sales which would take me away from home on a weekly basis. Rajah had become a great lovable brute of a dog. He was very protective of both Brenda and me. He was tolerant of strangers, if not friendly, and absolutely fearless, except with veterinarians. He was afraid of vets. Whenever he felt fear, he responded with aggressiveness. He was soon to become known as "the scourge of Vashon Island vets."

When it came time to take him for shots, I left Rajah in the suburban until I checked out the waiting room for aggressive dogs that might get into trouble with my dog. Discovering the coast was clear, I brought the dog into the waiting room. Rajah sat calm but very alert beside my left knee. I held him short on a choke chain.

The vet, a woman, entered and did a stupid thing. She appeared intimidated by him yet intent on dominating him. She dropped to one knee on the floor across the room and called out in a commanding voice, "Rajah. Is that my Rajah waiting for me?" He didn't like it. I never expected the vet to act with less than professional skill.

The dog lunged, barking loudly, and gnashed his fangs menacingly toward the vet. I held him back with some effort. I could feel his body trembling against mine. I knew he was afraid, but I didn't know why. Maybe it was the smell of the clinic. I never knew.

The vet stood and motioned me back to an exam room. Holding Rajah on a short leash, I followed her. Rajah was very nervous and tugged at the leash. Looking back, I understand it was a power play on the part of the veterinarian that failed. Why she needed that, I don't know. In any case, Tacoma's Proud Maharajah was not to be dominated.

The dog doctor administered the shots successfully to a very nervous dog I needed to hold tightly. When she had finished, she said some words to me. I can't remember the context of them and placed a hand on my shoulder. When she did, the dog jumped up and bit her forearm, not hard enough to break the skin but hard enough to bruise her and really anger her.

She pulled back, holding her arm, and shouted out, "If that was my dog, I'd beat him."

I struggled to control the dog. At the same time, I was shocked to hear this unprofessional outburst from her. I could only think to say, "Lady, be my guest." I offered her the leash. She dashed into another room and was gone. I paid the bill and beat a hasty retreat.

When I tried to put the dog in the back of the suburban, he insisted on climbing up onto the front seat. As I closed his door and went around to the driver's seat, he lay down beside me, his face between his paws, and mewled until I pulled the Chevy over and bent over to hug him close. He knew he had done a bad thing and he was very sorry for it.

He trembled.

I stroked his coat and said again and again that he was a good boy. "It'll be all right, Rajah, my sweet boy. Mama and I love you. We love you. You're my good boy."

Finally, he stopped trembling, licked my face, and we continued home.

"Honey, we're home," I called as I entered the house. "We gotta find a big steak for The Raj. He needs a max treat."

"Why, what happened," Brenda said as she stepped out into the hall.

"We better sit down. I'll tell you the whole story."

We went into the living room and sat together on the divan. Rajah followed, head and tail hanging. I didn't know how to reassure him. Brenda held his head in her hands as I told her what had happened.

"Oh, my sweet boy, it's all right," she crooned.

Before long, Rajah jumped up licked both our faces and attacked the steak waiting for him in his feeding bowl.

"It'll be all right now," Brenda said.

Next day, he seemed to have forgotten the incident, but he never was friendly toward another vet. Maybe he knew something we didn't.

20

We spent several wonderful years at what we called "the beach house." Because of deteriorating soil conditions that made us begin to worry that our high bank waterfront property might soon become low bank in the event of winter rain landslides, we looked to move to higher, more solid ground toward the center of Vashon or onto neighboring Maury Island. The two islands were joined by a causeway at the south end of Maury Island.

We found a house near the top of a gravelly hill on Maury Island at a place called Gold Beach. Our property was the farthest up the hill on solid ground away from the Sound. We moved in early 1994.

The former owner and builder of the house owned a cat. We expected Rajah, now a mature eight years old, to mark his territory, and we were right. Fortunately, this did not last long. The Raj moved in and took over his territory big time.

We built a chain-link fence around the backyard to give him room to roam and run. I wondered if six feet would be high enough, thinking of how he was able to jump after the Frisbee, but he understood the need of the fence and never tried to vault it. It was if he understood the fence was for keeping people out as much as keeping him inside. Besides, I took him for daily walks to satisfy his high energy level. Below our house was an abandoned gravel quarry where Rajah and I roamed freely every chance we had.

I always revolted by the sight a dog chained up. I think it goes against their nature. I'd hated to have to chain up The Bummer on military reservations. I believe that a chained up dog will wander whenever it gets free. We always raised our dogs as house dogs and tried to give them room to run and stretch their muscles.

The years passed uneventfully as Rajah grew older. He enjoyed his domain in the backyard and only grew upset when the occasional squirrel invaded his privacy.

On evenings, we'd spread out on a sectional lounge and watch television in the large room we called "the stadium." It held a woodstove and a wet bar, and on the walls, we displayed our favorite Washington Husky football pictures. During those years, the Huskies were in top of form, and we attended every home game.

We'd relax together on the sectional; Rajah sprawled between Brenda and me, just enjoying the peace and quiet of Maury Island. One night as we relaxed there, a commercial about Alaska appeared on the tube. There were wolves howling in it. All at once, Rajah joined in and began to howl with the wolves on the screen. I joined in and howled along with the dog. The more I howled, the more and louder Rajah howled, lifting his nose toward the ceiling. Brenda joined us, and we three howled like we were members of the pack. Whatever the neighbors could hear or might think of this primeval concert, we neither knew nor cared. After that, we held nearly nightly howling sessions.

Chris wrote of one Christmas on Mauri Island, gently edited: *I loved Christmases when I got to spend a few days with my folks at the Gold Beach House. One holiday, I had been given an electric putting machine. Hit the ball into the hole and it would be bounced back by the machine. It was great fun, and I spent an hour playing with it after all the presents had been handed out. Rajah watched me closely the whole time from his favorite spot on the sectional. Later, Mom began cooking dinner. I learned early on the advantages of keeping her company in the kitchen. I think some of my best quality time spent with Mom was with her in the kitchen. While we talked, I heard a noise in the stadium. Thwock! Thump, thump, thump. Thwock! Thump, thump, thump. I knew Dad was in the basement working on a project. I walked into the stadium and found a ramped up Rajah picking up a ball in his mouth and dropping it into the putting machine causing them to be shot out and he then chased them down. I wished I had a camera to take pictures. I'll never forget the sight of Rajah operating the putting machine. It was amazing, entertaining, funny, and ingenious. I'll always remember*

Rajah for his physical strength and ability as well as his intelligence. I don't think I ever saw another dog with his problem solving ability.

When it came time for the dog to have shots again, I took him to the one remaining vet on the islands who had not met my scourge of Vashon, Dr. Larry Glickstein. He was a little skinny guy with a reputation for being kicked by horses and such, but my first and lasting impression of him was that he loved animals and he knew his stuff.

On the day of the appointment, I parked my SUV, a Jeep Cherokee now, outside the clinic and, leaving the dog outside in the back of the Jeep, went inside to see if they had a muzzle that might fit Rajah. Several were proffered, and I picked the one that appeared to be the right size. I went outside and, opening the rear hatch on the Jeep, started to fit the muzzle on Rajah. He objected just a little. Dr. Glickstein appeared unexpectedly behind me.

"This dog doesn't look vicious to me. He doesn't need a muzzle. Bring him on inside."

"Are you sure, Doc? He's afraid of vets and has bitten nearly every other one on the island."

"He'll be fine. Don't bother with the muzzle. Just bring him on in."

I snapped on Rajah's lead, and together, we entered the clinic. I was nervous, and I guess the dog sensed my feelings. Dr. Glickstein was waiting at the front desk. It was then that he made his mistake. Dropping to one knee, Dr. Larry reached out to Rajah. When he did, Rajah bit him on the forearm. It wasn't a nip or a snap. Rajah bit him right to the bone. Grasping his arm with his other hand, Larry disappeared into the rear of the clinic. Hastily, I put the dog back into the Jeep.

I returned alone inside to wait and see what the doctor's pronouncement would be. I felt terrible. I wondered what I would do for vet service from now on. I'd used up my options for treatment on the island.

Nearly an hour later, Larry reappeared, acting as if nothing had happened. "I'll continue to treat your dog, but from now on, you'll need to use the muzzle. Bring him in for his shots."

"Gosh, Doc, I'm really sorry. I should have warned you about getting down to his level. He doesn't like that."

Retrieving the muzzle, I went back out to bring Rajah in for his shots. The dog had decided the vet was not his friend and protested so much I had to hold him close to my chest and try to block his view of the doc administering the needle.

The next year, Doctor Larry told me I should have Rajah neutered.

"Doc, you're not saying this just to get even with my dog, are you?"

"Of course not, Dick. I see he has gained some weight, and I think his temperament will mellow if we relieve him of his gonads. You don't plan to offer him out to stud at his age, do you?"

"No."

"Then neutering will help him to age more gracefully and mellow out."

On the appointed day, I arrived at the clinic and went inside alone to get a muzzle for the dog.

Dr. Larry came out from the lab and said, "Rather than get him all upset, I think it will be better if I administer a sedative to him while he's still in the vehicle."

"Fine, just give me a few minutes to get the muzzle on him and get a good grip on his head before you come out."

I sat on the rear deck of the Jeep and placed a muzzle on Rajah. Cradling him in my arms, I petted him and talked to him in an attempt to sooth him. He was just settling down when Larry appeared. I could feel the dog tense, and he began to growl. I held him tighter as Larry administered the sedative in one foreleg.

"There, let him settle down a while, and we'll take him into the operating room."

I sat there with The Raj. I stroked his cheek and crooned to him, "That's my good boy. Everything's going to be fine. My good, good boy."

Larry returned. Rajah growled a low menacing growl.

"He doesn't seem to have quieted down," I said.

"I'll prepare another shot for him. He's a big boy."

Larry administered another shot to Rajah, and as I held him tightly in my arms, he went suddenly limp. I was reminded of how I'd felt when Bummer went limp with death. Larry saw this reaction at the same moment. "He's not breathing. I'll get a blanket."

I panicked. We placed Rajah's body on the blanket and rushed him into the clinic where we placed him onto an operating table. The doctor attached some apparatus to the dog's body with the aid of an assistant. He administered another shot.

"Ahhh. He's breathing again. He'll be fine now. Dick, you go home. Come back in about four hours. Don't worry. I'll take good care of him."

I drove the short distance to my house and kept busy the four hours, trying not to worry. The few seconds when Rajah had stopped breathing had left me shaken and nervous. When the time had passed, I hurried back to the clinic and found the dog zonked on the floor of a large cage. I stooped and managed to reach his muzzle to stroke it with my fingers, whispering words of praise and encouragement all the while. Rajah stirred and licked my fingers. When he growled and curled his lip, I knew the vet had entered the room. I knew too that Rajah would never forgive him for taking his cojones. Larry treated the dog for the rest of the animal's life and never once mentioned Rajah's dislike for him or the time he had been bitten by the dog.

Rajah lived out the rest of his life in comfort at our island home. If we expected his operation to mellow him, we were mistaken, for only with members of our family was he gentle and loving. I never worried about Brenda's safety during my frequent travels off island to the many places in western North America and Canada where my job called me. Rajah was always close by her side. He could handle any threat. He slept under our bed at night. We often heard him padding through the house on security rounds at night. We had grown inured to the German shepherd tendency toward nighttime flatulence. Rajah often took the heat for my own tendency in that arena. Often in the stadium, I'd let one go and say under my breath, "Bad dog." Rajah never objected, but my family soon got wind literally of my ploy, and from then on, I took the heat, whichever of us were guilty.

One day, while working in our rock garden adjacent to our deck behind the house, Rajah inadvertently stepped into the crack between a large granite boulder and the surface of the deck. I wasn't home, and Brenda later told me of her efforts to extricate the dog from his foot trap. His struggles resulted in permanent injury to his right hindfoot so that ever afterward his nighttime hallway patrolling could be heard as he dragged his right hindfoot.

In July 1999, we decided it was time to put Rajah down. He had lived a good life of fourteen years but had grown feeble and could no longer climb the stairs. He needed help getting aboard the Jeep. He'd put his front feet up, and I'd lift the rear portion of his 120 pounds onto the deck of the vehicle. As time went by, he couldn't even manage that. He still had that regal walk except now it was very slow. We didn't want him to have to live in pain. Chris lived in Everett, Washington, now and was working on the Boeing flight line. I called and told him it was time. We agreed on a day when he'd be available to come home.

I called the vet and explained the situation. Larry offered to come to our house and put Rajah to sleep there. I thought that was extraordinarily kind of him, especially considering the dog's animosity toward him.

I made preparations for a proper funeral for Tacoma's Proud Maharajah. I picked a shady spot among some trees in the backyard where people seldom went. I dug a deep grave the size of a steamer trunk I'd decided to use as a casket. Brenda offered up a blanket to use as a shroud. We spread it on the garage floor.

As the time drew near, both Chris and Dr. Larry had arrived. Chris and I walked Rajah. He healed on command automatically now, out the back door and around the house to the garage door which was open. Rajah could no longer walk down the stairs from the front of the house to the garage, so we made a kind of a last parade for him around the house. The dog stopped at the corner of the house and looked back toward the deck where Brenda stood. She couldn't bear to go down to the garage. The Raj looked at her for a long moment. His eyes held a look I remembered from Little Joe in the jungles of Vietnam.

We continued on to the garage. If the dog knew Larry was there, he didn't show it. Moving to the blanket, I gave my last order to Rajah. "Down." He sat painfully and settled onto the center of the blanket. Sniffing at what was to become his shroud, I knew he detected the scents of Brenda and me on it.

I knelt beside him and gathered him in my arms, my tears wetting his pelt. I had thought to muzzle him but couldn't bear to. I held him more to comfort him than to restrain him. The dog looked up into my eyes and held the gaze until his eyes glazed over in death.

I can't remember when Larry left, but sometime later, I let go of Rajah's now limp body and wrapped him tightly in the blanket. With Chris's help, I placed him gently into the trunk, which would serve as his final bed. Beside him, I placed his favorite Frisbee, now chewed full of holes. We shut and locked the trunk and then carried it to the backyard and placed it on two poles across the tomb I'd prepared. Brenda joined us, and the three of us bade farewell to a proud dog as, with ropes, Chris and I lowered the trunk slowly into the ground.

I thought of each of my dogs and felt their spirits around me. Little Joe, Snake, and Bummer surrounded the grave and welcomed the soul of Rajah into their midst. Their spirits would be with me as long as I remembered them, which would mean always.

Working together slowly, Chris and I covered the casket with earth. Later, I planted a rhododendron on the grave to discourage future owners of the property from digging it up.

21

Christmas 1999 was a bittersweet time for us. Two of our three children, Evelyn and Chris, would spend the holidays with us. At the same time, we were still mourning Rajah who slept the long sleep in the backyard. I spent a few minutes daily, whenever I was at home, tending his grave. Brenda had loved the dog as much as I and, when we discussed getting another dog, agreed to wait until we were ready to commit to another close relationship with a dog. I thought I'd need at least a year. We felt there could never be another Tacoma's Proud Maharajah. We were right, except we were not prepared for what the community of dog spirits had in store for us.

My own grieving for Rajah was as strong and as lasting as it had been for The Bummer, but at least I had had closure with The Raj. I always felt I'd deserted Bummer because I left him to be cremated and hadn't even claimed the ashes. I had taken Rajah to the end of his life and kept him close. I thanked Dr. Larry Glickstein for that.

One evening, soon after the dog's burial, Brenda and I had made what I thought was a final decision. She approached me in the stadium and put her arms around me. "Dick, sweetheart, I know how much you loved that dog. I know no other dog can ever take his place or replace the love you feel for him, but I think it's time you moved on. I know you need a dog in your life."

"Maybe you're right. Maybe I do need another dog. Maybe next year. Right now, I can't even think about it. I loved Rajah. I know you loved him too. If I ever agree to have another dog, I don't want it to be an aggressive, confrontational dog like our last two. I want it to be mellow like a golden retriever, and I want it to be a female."

A few days before Christmas, our younger daughter Evelyn was due to fly in to Sea-Tac Airport from Anchorage. I planned to meet her there. Sometime in the midmorning, she called. "My plane is super late. I've called Chris, and he'll pick me up at the airport on his way down from Everett."

That was fine with me. I never looked forward to the long ferry lines and long waits at the airport. "That's fine, sweetheart. We'll be waiting for you."

Later, Chris called. "Evelyn needs to do some Christmas shopping. I'm taking her by the Tacoma Mall on the way home. We should be there in time for supper."

"Okay, son. Drive carefully. We're having a late supper anyway."

When they finally arrived, Evelyn carrying a brown shopping bag, we met them at the door and exchanged hugs and kisses.

"Here, Dad. Hold my bag while I take my coat off."

"Sure." I took the bag.

Something was amiss. The bag was moving. I looked down into it into a pair of soft, chestnut-colored eyes. A fuzzy golden-colored puppy gazed up at me with large trusting eyes.

"What?"

Around her neck (somehow, I knew she was a female), she wore a crimson Christmas bow. I was shocked—no, enthralled—no, entranced by this beautiful golden puppy. I reached into the bag and grasped her in my arms, dropping the bag to the floor.

"What." I was speechless.

I held her closely. She gazed into my eyes with trusting confidence. Gently, she licked my nose. There was no fear or trepidation in her.

I looked up at my family standing around and realized I was the victim of a family conspiracy. "Merry Christmas," they all shouted and gathered round my pup and me for kisses all around.

We gathered around the tree for one of the happiest Christmases ever.

"What shall we call her?"

All knew I had accepted her as my own true love.

"I think a good name for her would be Chloe," Brenda said.

I held the pup up at eye level, looked deep into her chestnut eyes, and said, "Chloe it shall be."

Later, to satisfy AKC rules, we registered her as "Maury's Golden Chloe."

Chloe was from the beginning a loving arm full of gold—warm, silky gold. She fitted in both my hands and weighed not more than two or three pounds. But her eyes said it all. Her eyes were so full of love it made my heart sing.

That night, I held on my lap by the fire and sang.

> Chloe is the girl for me
> Always knew that she would be.
> Though she doesn't know my name
> I will play the waiting game.
> Chloe, she's the girl for me.

She gazed up at me as if to say, "Oh, that is so beautiful. Has there ever been anyone who could sing a sweeter song? Are you singing just for me?"

I had a fan club of one. She settled in my lap and went to sleep.

Evelyn said, "Her mother had the litter in a barn and, each morning, took her pups outside to do their business. So she's totally housebroken."

"Right."

On the first night, we spread newspapers in all the likely places. I followed her about, keeping close watch as she explored her new surroundings. When time for bed came around and she still hadn't made to relieve herself, I took her out into the backyard. I crooned to her and softly persuaded her to do what all puppies must ultimately do. When she finally squatted demurely in the grass, I praised her mightily as I picked her up in my arms and rushed indoors to share the good news with Brenda.

"Oh, what a good girl our Chloe is. Look, honey, at our great good golden girl, our Chloe."

The pup relaxed in my arms, tongue hanging out and looking at us as if to say, "What's the big deal?"

During the night, we didn't pen her up. We placed her on a towel under the edge of our bed. She chose always to sleep as close to Brenda as she could get. We tried letting her sleep between us but were afraid one of us would crush her in our sleep. As well, she seemed to prefer the floor. Later, we bought a dog mattress for her.

Early the next morning, Brenda was awakened by the puppy's crying from somewhere outside our bedroom. Jumping up, she ran out to discover Chloe at the head of the stairs, wanting to go down, but unable to negotiate the distance between the steps. Brenda picked her up and hurried down to the back door, placing her gently on the turf. Chloe wasted no time before she squatted and relieved herself.

22

Chloe settled in easily as a member of the family. Her disposition was 180 degrees out from those of our previous dogs. She was gentle and affectionate where my other dogs had been independent and aggressive. While the others had looked into my eyes and communicated a desire to make me understand why and who they were, Chloe looked at me with understanding and unquestioning love. She never asked how smart I thought she was but conveyed with her wise look, "How smart you are?" or "Why didn't I think of that?"

She grew quickly into a most beautifully golden-haired young dog. At eighty-five pounds, she was big for a female retriever but that she was a female, there was no doubt, and there was no doubt that she knew it. She developed a seductive walk that I had never seen on any dog before. When she strolled across the lawn, her walk reminded me of a canine Ava Gardner, swinging her hips and inviting onlookers to admire her beauty. Don't get me wrong. She wasn't vain. She was just the opposite—she loved people. She loved us. She wanted only to love and to be loved.

She was even-tempered and eager to please. She'd bark whenever a stranger showed up at the house, and that was a good thing, but her approach to a new face was a rush of affection for a new friend.

She loved to cuddle on the floor with Brenda or me or the both of us in front of the TV in the evenings.

I didn't have to take her to obedience school as I had The Raj. She just naturally picked up on all the commands and was eager to obey. Commands to obey were more to her like invitations. In short, she was the most lovable dog we'd ever had in our family. She was quick to adapt and soon became a necessary member of our clan.

During that time, I managed a sales force marketing low vision devices to eye care professionals engaged in rehabilitating the visually impaired. I was attuned to Chloe's special skills. I recognized her as a candidate to be a guide dog or at least a companion dog. I knew she would qualify in any field within the discipline. Selfishly, I kept her for my own family. Later, I was glad I had.

"Oh, my Chloe puppy. Oh, my best dog. How I love my Chloe." These words were the way I talked to her all her life. She would come close and look deeply into my eyes with those beautiful chestnut-colored eyes of hers and say, not in words, "I can see how you love me. As you love me, so do I love you."

A friend of Phil McClure's had moved onto the island. He was, like Phil, a retired Green Beret but a major general. His name was Harley Davis. I went over to his house soon after he and his wife moved in to help him do something—I can't remember what. He owned two dogs, or should I say, he had two dogs in his house. One was a fairly large, curly-haired terrier that was very energetic. The other I discovered peeking shyly out from under an end table. Automatically, I dropped to one knee and reached out to let the dog smell my open palm and, when she accepted me, rub the dog's head.

"That's Kelly," the general said. "She belongs to my son. We're taking care of her for him while he looks for a new place to live. We're looking for a home for her. She doesn't get along very well with our dog. My son rescued her from a dumpster in Tacoma a few months ago."

The dog looked like a Border Collie mix but smaller and very shy. I could see she hid from the boisterous terrier that was all over the house.

"Let me show you around my new digs," Harley said, leading me out the back door. I noticed Kelly followed us or maybe me. As I followed General Davis around his property, he talked incessantly about his plans for developing the new property. I paid more attention to Kelly who followed everywhere at my heels.

"The dog seems attracted to you. Wouldn't you like to take her home with you?"

"Yes, I would, but I already have a dog. I can't handle two. But I might know someone who would like her. I'll check and let you know."

I was thinking of Chris who was living alone in an apartment in Everett. *He loved dogs and would like Kelly*, I thought.

That evening, I called my son and told him about this dog and how she was forced to live in fear of a larger, more active dog.

"How old is she?"

"Dunno. Maybe five or six. She's a sweet, affectionate thing."

"I'll come down next weekend and take a look at her. You'll set it up?"

"Sure. Plan on having dinner with us."

"Will there be beer?"

"There will be beer."

"Count me in."

I called Harley Davis and arranged for Chris to see the dog the following Sunday.

I met Chris at the ferry, and we drove south on the island to the Davis house. When Harley opened the door, Kelly rushed to me and looked up, little tongue hanging out. She whimpered. I knelt and petted her. "Son, this is Kelly."

That was all it took. Chris adopted Kelly and took her home.

The following year, Chris had gotten married and moved in with his wife in Tacoma. She came with a ready-made family of two children from two fathers, neither of which was married to the mother.

I had a serious talk with my son.

"Chris, are you sure this woman is the one you want to marry?"

"I love her, Dad."

So that was that. I worried about Kelly's treatment by the new children.

"Surely, you don't plan to stay here on the Tacoma hilltop, do you, son?"

The hilltop area of Tacoma was basically a slum area and the high crime area of the city.

"No, of course not. What I'd really like to do is build a home on Maury or Vashon close to you and with a couple of acres of land."

"I'll look around."

There was nothing available on Vashon Island, no plots of two acres for sale with two adjacent plots. I began to widen my search until I found ideal acreage on the Key Peninsula. I selected two 2-½ acre lots abutting a marine state park.

And so it was, we built homes next to each other. Kelly and Chloe visited often and grew to be great pals. Both were laid back dogs, so they loved to hang out together. Kelly turned out to be older than we thought. When Chris had a son, our grandson, Kelly began to take short shrift in the attention department. The dog loved Chris but in his absence turned to me.

Lakebay, on the Key Peninsula, introduced us to a whole new way of life. We enjoyed space, the deep woods, and the saltwater of Puget Sound within walking distance. Chloe settled in nicely, except for the first few days when she wouldn't relieve herself on the bare ground around the house, no grass having taken root yet. She would circle and circle but couldn't find any grass on which to go. Then nature took its course, and she took charge of the property.

During the next couple of years, Chloe continued to mature into a beautiful adult retriever. We had her neutered by Dr. Cynthia Pope, who became our family veterinarian in Purdy, Washington, thirteen miles away at the head of the Key Peninsula. Dr. Pope was a fine and caring vet who liked Chloe very much. She'd always spend time grooming and playing with the dog.

Chris managed to hang on at Boeing for another year before opting to sign on seagoing tugs again. That meant long cruises away from home. Kelly spent longer times with us. None of the children seemed to care for her very much. Brenda and I grew to love her. She knew it and responded to our care. Chris's wife couldn't stand the long separations and filed for divorce. Chris left the house and asked us to care for Kelly until he could get his stuff together. Of course, we agreed, and the dog came to live with us. The two dogs became close, almost inseparable friends. They did everything together.

After a few months, Kelly began to falter. She seemed in almost constant joint pain and slept a lot more.

"I think you're going to have to put her down very soon," I said during one of Chris's visits between stints at sea. He agreed sadly.

"Let's wait a little while and see if she improves."

She didn't improve but got worse. It hurt us to see her obvious and constant discomfort. When Chris came home again, I told him it was definitely time to put Kelly to sleep.

With an aching heart, he took her to the vet who gave her a shot. Chris brought her home and buried her in the woods behind his house.

Chloe mourned for Kelly along with the rest of us. I tried to spend more time with her. I bought a Frisbee and threw it for her as I had done for Rajah, but she never got the hang of catching it on the fly. She'd let it land and then dutifully retrieve it. After a while, I gave it up for almost daily walks along the beach. She loved that and would walk for miles with me, staying at the heel.

I tried to interest her in going for a swim, but she wasn't having any of that. I pondered the situation wherein a retriever didn't like to swim but finally accepted it as a win-win situation. If she didn't want to get wet, then I wouldn't have to comb the wet sand out of her coat. She seemed perfectly satisfied with the role of constant companion to Brenda while I was gone on my many business trips. After she had gotten over missing Kelly, she was completely content when the three of us were together.

23

As we grew older together, Chloe at a more rapid rate than me, though we were all three getting gray around the muzzle, Chloe taught me some things about dogs.

Chloe was just as glad to see me when I returned from a trip to the garage as she was when I returned from my many weeklong business trips. Dogs seem to have no sense of the passage of time. They only know joy when we are with them. When we are gone, they wait for our return. They know when we go and when we come back. We are present equals happy; we are absent equals sad. They have no sense of the passage of time.

To test this idea, I asked Chloe if she wanted to go for a ride. She loved riding in the car or truck and was accustomed to riding with me each morning the three miles down to home to get the daily paper. Often, we travelled the several more miles into Key Center and the grocery store. This time, her ride was from the driveway into the garage. She dismounted as happy as if we gone to town and back. As we walked into the house, I could see she was perfectly satisfied. A few more repetitions and I got into the habit of inviting her aboard whenever I had to move the car—worked for her; worked for me.

Pondering this revelation and others about dogs I had known, I thought about the commandments of God and thought about how my canine companions lived up to the ultimate word.

God said, first, we should have no other gods before him. He said we should not carve idols and should not bow down before them. While I wasn't too sure about our dogs' view of us in their hierarchy, it appeared that while they almost worshipped their human companions, still there was something in their demeanor that seemed to indicate a knowledge or at least a recognition of a higher power.

"You shall not take the name of the Lord Your God in vain, for the Lord will not leave unpunished him who takes His name in vain." No problem there. I never heard a dog take the name of the Lord in vain, though I have sometimes seen an expression in their faces which seemed to say, "No."

"Remember to keep holy the Sabbath day." It seems to me every day in a dog's day is kept holy. Chloe worshipped each day for what it was. When it rained, she rushed out to take glory in each day with me. When the sun shone, she rushed out to take in and share its glory with Brenda and me.

"Honor your mother and father." While I don't believe any of my dogs remembered their parents, they certainly honored Brenda and me as their parents. They knew no others.

"You shall not kill." One time when we were returning together after a walk through the woods and down to the beach, Chloe veered away from her normal heel position at my left and nosed into the bushes. When she returned to me, she had a small floppy-eared bunny in her mouth. She offered it up to me. When I accepted it, she licked the little bunny and my hand. Thinking about the retriever's penchant for doing no harm, I thought of Snake and decided he'd need special dispensation. I thought about all my dogs and how gentle Chloe was in comparison to all the rest.

"You shall not commit adultery." Not sure this applies to dogs. Nor do the rest of the commandments. I never knew a dog to steal, covet, or bear false witness. Oh, I remember bummer once stole a fish, but he'd been forgiven for that many years before.

My dogs measured up more stringently to God's commandments than any living human I knew. They were as totally innocent as the animals that lived in the garden of Eden. They never did anything to subvert their original essence with the angels. They live today as God created them, neither bad nor good but simply to glorify our Father in heaven.

Chloe was much more sensitive to our moods than the other dogs had been, maybe not so different but more pronounced. She had strong feelings and would sulk if she felt slighted and readily forgive when we worked to correct our failings. Whenever Brenda and I argued, which was fairly frequently, Chloe stood between us and cried out for us to stop the nonsense and just love each other as she loved us.

One evening, the three of us sat together watching television. Chloe usually went to sleep at our feet. This night was different. She paid a lot of attention to Brenda, kept putting her head in Brenda's lap and prodding under her arms with her nose. Around ten o'clock, Brenda said to me, "Dick, I feel strange. I think you'd better take me to the hospital."

Brenda avoided hospitals whenever possible. I got up and put my shoes on. I didn't question her judgment but went outside to get the car out of the garage. I drove the thirty-five miles to the Bremerton Naval Hospital as fast as I dared in the dark.

We entered the emergency room where attendants put her on a gurney. A nurse hooked Brenda up to the apparatus, which would monitor her vital signs, and a doctor began to examine her. They found nothing wrong with her, and I sat next to her watching the dials register her apparent well-being. Around midnight, I said, "Honey, are you ready to go home?"

"I sure am if I can just get freed from all these pins and needles."

At just about 2:00 a.m., Brenda suffered a massive heart attack. She survived it, thanks to warnings from Chloe that resulted in Brenda's being under immediate aid at the time of her attack. We both credited the dog with saving Brenda's life. If Chloe hadn't been so persistent with Brenda, she might have had the attack at home and would surely have died.

Brenda lives today with several steel stents throughout her body, including two in her heart. I call her the six-million-dollar woman. We are both thankful to Chloe who lived another two years and then died of cancer. I buried her on the hill in front of our house and plant flowers each spring on her grave. I know her soul abides in heaven or at least in our hearts.

24

Unlike when Rajah died and we didn't want another dog right away, Brenda and I felt an immediate need to replace Chloe with another golden retriever. We needed the love and attention they gave us. I turned to the Internet and discovered a golden retriever rescue network. I informed them of our need for a dog.

Two days later, I got a call from the Tacoma Animal Rescue Center informing me they had a golden retriever that had recently been rescued and would soon be ready for adoption. I responded immediately and drove the fifteen miles to the rescue center to see the dog. I knew a golden would be quickly snapped up.

Arriving at the center, a woman attendant took me to the dog's kennel, but it was empty. I feared the dog had already been claimed. "Oh no. She's still here. They've just moved her. We'll find her. No fear."

We walked down the aisles, dogs barking incessantly, hopeful faces staring at us as we passed. "Ah, here she is."

I stood before a large cage and looked at a golden dog sitting forlorn and bedraggled in the center of the cage. I looked at her doubtfully. She returned my look hopefully. She looked rather small for a golden.

"How old do you think she is?"

"We estimate about one year old."

"How did you obtain her?"

"We found her roaming the streets in Tacoma. Apparently, she'd been wandering for some time. She was dirty and hungry. We cleaned her up and gave her a grooming. She's due to be neutered later today."

There was that ugly word—*neuter*. I knew it had to be done.

"Then you plan not to kill her?"

"We haven't killed an animal here for the last five years. Our director won't allow it."

"Can I go in the cage?" I was still studying the dog as she studied me.

"Of course. Her name is Sandy." The attendant let me into the cell. I knelt before the dog and took her head in both my hands. She responded by licking my hands. After studying her for several minutes, I leaned over and kissed her forehead. She licked my nose. Her tongue was so soft. I turned to the attendant. She was crying. I didn't know why. "I want this dog. What do I have to do?"

"Come. I'll take you to fill out the paperwork. If all is well, Sandy will be ready to leave in two days."

All went well. I requested she have a chip. Chris and I drove down to the rescue center two days later to pick up the dog. I put her on a lead and started to walk out with her. She strained at the lead pulling me along and seeming to know which car was mine. I opened the back of Brenda's Subaru Outback, and she leapt aboard, apparently anxious to be gone from her captivity.

Sandy seemed perfectly at home in the car. I left the leash on her because I feared she would bolt, given the chance, as she might have before. When we arrived at the house, we let her out of the car on her leash, and she responded to my every movement with the cord. I brought her into the house, and she immediately settled in. She loved Brenda. She needed no housebreaking. In the eight years we've had her now, she always waits to be let out in the morning to relieve her bladder and later afternoon to clear her bowels outside.

I took her to see my vet who gave her a good going over and found her healthy. "Oh, I see she's got white stockings. She's not purebred golden retriever."

I didn't care. I loved her as she was. She was full grown at seventy pounds. Her tail was curled and white-tipped. She ran very fast for a golden. She loved everybody who came in contact with her.

One day, several years after Sandy came to live with us, we were watching the annual Westminster Dog Show from back east. We loved to watch the working dog session. The winner of that year's working dog competition was a beautiful Nova Scotia Duck Toler Retriever.

"Look, honey. That dog looks just like Sandy."

She agreed and we did some research that revealed our dog was indeed a Duck Toler. That answered a lot of questions, including our dog's short coat and her ability to run so fast.

I had been forced to retire and care for Brenda. Lots of down time and I began writing stories. Since 2007, I have managed an average of one book per year. This will be number 10. The books are like my children. Someone recently asked me at a book show, which was my favorite. "That's like asking me which of my children is my favorite. I created them, and I love them all. Through them, I will live forever."

Sandy is about eight years old now. Before very much longer, she'll be joining Chloe on the hill. Until that time, she's a great comfort to Brenda and me. I believe someday, her soul will continue to give us comfort with the rest of our dogs in heaven.

End Story

These then have been and are the stories of my dogs. Their spirits surround me as I write. Tears cloud my eyes as I think of each of them. They will remain with me for whatever time I have left on this earth and then welcome me into the hereafter. I have been blessed to have known them.

That the dog I saw during combat operations in Vietnam was Little Joe is speculative. I only saw him momentarily. But the spark of recognition that passed between us convinced me this was my Joe. Casualty records from the Seventh Cavalry at the battle of the Ia Drang River list among those KIA, a scout dog named Blackie. The dates coincide with the time I encountered him.

The facts of some of Snake's exploits against the enemy and at least one instance of having saved my life are documented in service logs and after-action reports. I learned from retired Lieutenant Colonel Rick Nelson in 1986, then Captain Nelson, that after I left Kon Tum, our advisory team was involved in action resulting in obliteration of most of the team including the brave little black dog we called Snake.

My association with these two dogs prepared me to understand the wild heart of Bummer. He was a child of winter. He loved the snow and was most comfortable when the temperature fell into the single numbers. I was able to keep Bummer close to me all his life. For that, I am grateful.

Pride in my Rajah must have shown through in my account of his life. I have his picture and his one blue ribbon hanging on the wall beside my bed. He loved our family and was true to us unto death. He was a handsome brute with the courage of my previous canine companions. He was always gentle with the children and stood first in line to fight for dominance over other dogs. He and I shared his years on earth with joy. I thank God for that.

Chloe brought great comfort to our latter years. She had a great heart and once bravely faced down a bear in the backyard yet was always a gentle lap dog in the house. That she saved Brenda's life that one night is indisputable. I still mourn her absence and feel the essence of her love and loyalty.

Sandy brings an energy that gets me up and out on a frosty morning to go for a brisk walk through the neighborhood or in the woods. She is gentle and loves to cuddle with me on the floor or on her "blankie." She spends a lot of time sleeping now as she grows older. God bless her as he has blessed us with the lives of our dogs.

> Sandy is the girl for me,
> always knew that she would be.
> Though she doesn't know my name,
> I will play the waiting game.
> Sandy—she's the girl for me.

Epilogue

Today, Christmas Day 2017, I'm sitting before the fireplace thinking of my dogs. I like to think Brenda and I and Sandy are growing older together and gracefully, although Brenda claims I am unable to do it gracefully.

If not gracefully, then I can do it with contentment that all my children have become dog lovers. Cindy, my oldest, keeps two bull mastiffs in her home in Houston, Texas. One of them, a rescue dog, has just been diagnosed with cancer. He's given two months to live. By the condition of his jaws, his upper and lower fangs ground down mercilessly, the vet thinks he was formerly used as a bait dog for pit fighting. Whatever pain he went through when he was younger, at least he has lived a life of comfort and love with Cindy. I love her for that.

Evelyn, my middle child, in her fifties now and recently widowed, keeps a pair of pit bull mix dogs at her home in Skipperville, Alabama.

Chris, my favorite (my only) son, lives within five miles of our house and keeps two rescue dogs. One of them a big rangy shepherd mix we call bear and the other a Chihuahua mix. I call them Mutt and Jeff.

All together, we are a happy, dog-loving family and looking forward to eternal life by the grace of our Lord Jesus, the Christ, and shared with the spirits of our dogs.

About the Author

Richard A. M. Dixon is a retired U.S. Army officer and decorated combat infantry leader who served with distinction for more than twenty years. He was educated at the University of Washington and received a BS in psychology. Later, he was awarded a MS in military science and history.

He began writing full time in 2007 and has published nine books, mostly historic fiction. He won a prize in a national competition in 2014 for his memoir, *Angels in My Foxhole*. He received excellent reviews by the US Review of Books for his 2016 historic novel, *The Tiger of Dien Bien Phu.*

He lives in the woods on Puget Sound, Washington, with his wife and his dog Sandy.

CPSIA information can be obtained
at www.ICGtesting.com
Printed in the USA
FSHW021420161118
53786FS